The Soaps

DAYTIME SERIALS OF RADIO AND TV

BY MADELEINE EDMONDSON AND DAVID ROUNDS

STEIN AND DAY/*Publishers*/New York

ACKNOWLEDGMENTS

Grateful acknowledgment is extended to the following people and organizations: Bill Behanna, A.C. Nielsen Co.; K.R. Baumbusch, John F. Murray Advertising Agency; Robert Carrington; Columbia Broadcasting System; John Desmond; Daisy Edmondson; Patricia Carrington Ephron; Don Ettlinger; Joseph Hardy; National Broadcasting Company; Virginia Payne; James B. Poteat, Television Information Office; Maxwell Silverman, Theater Collection, New York Public Library at Lincoln Center; Clarke Taylor; Elizabeth Wasik Thompson; Roy Winsor

The voice I hear this passing night was heard
In ancient days by emperor and clown . . .
The same that oft-times hath
Charm'd magic casements, opening on the foam
Of perilous seas, in faery lands forlorn.

For my parents
—David

For Frank, with love
—Madeleine

CONTENTS

ILLUSTRATIONS

The Soaps

THE SOAPSCAPE

§

Dr. Louis I. Berg, a New York psychiatrist and writer, was a man who hated soaps. Ironically, his name lives on today only because of its association with the form he so despised.

Dr. Berg's crusade against soap opera began in 1941, when he developed the suspicion that certain symptoms manifested by his patients, certain disturbing relapses, might have their origin in addiction to radio serials. Setting out to test his hypothesis that such symptoms as tachycardia, arrhythmia, emotional instability, and vertigo might be produced by soap opera, he found just what he had set out to look for. After a daily dose of two leading exemplars, *Right to Happiness* and *Woman in White,* Dr. Berg tested his own blood pressure and found it rising.

Serials, he concluded on this evidence, are dangerous, especially to the middle-aged woman, the adolescent, and the neurotic. They furnish to those unfortunate addicts "the same release for the emotionally distorted that is supplied to those who derive satisfaction from a lynching bee, who lick their lips at the salacious scandals of a *crime passionnel,* who in the unregretted past cried out in ecstasy at a witch burning."

The subject of all this tempestuous verbiage was then, as now, a humble art form, meek and unconfident, looked down upon by the cultivated and even sometimes by its own creators. But though it has often been snubbed and publicly humiliated, it has always been beloved by millions who have found it indispensable to their private well-being.

What is it, then, that can arouse such fierce loyalties in its audience and such intemperate opposition from its critics? The dictionary defines it as "a radio or television serial drama performed usu. on a daytime commercial program and chiefly characterized by stock domestic situations and often melodramatic or sentimental treatment."

There is also James Thurber's famous definition, more often quoted but considerably less helpful: "A soap opera is a kind of sandwich, whose recipe is simple enough, although it took years to compound. Between thick slices of advertising, spread twelve minutes of dialogue, add predicament, villainy, and female suffering in equal measure, throw in a dash of nobility, sprinkle with tears, season with organ music, cover with a rich announcer sauce, and serve five times a week."

But the truth is that nobody needs a definition. Everyone recognizes soap opera instantly, on television, radio, or in everyday life—presumably someone else's. Even people whose knowledge of soaps is limited to what they could pick up when a bad cold or measles kept them at home on a youthful weekday seem to have taken it in like so many dry sponges and to have held on to it like grim death.

From that brief childhood exposure they remember how Stella Dallas went out of her daughter Laurel's life forever—and then popped back in again whenever it seemed advisable. They recall the sufferings of Mary Noble, married to one of Broadway's most handsome and successful actors, and her fears that she would never be able to keep her husband's love, tempted as he naturally was by all those beautiful actresses he spent his working life with. And Our Gal Sunday . . . could that simple girl from a small mining town in the West ever find happiness with a rich and titled Englishman? Would Young Widder Brown's children ever break down and permit her to wed Dr. Anthony Loring?

People who remembered all this could laugh when Bob and Ray came along with *Mary Backstayge, Noble Wife* and *One Feller's Family,* which always ended with the announcer saying, "*One Feller's Family* is written and directed by T. Wilson Messy. This has been a Messy Production." In 1960 the last of the radio soaps left the air. Three years later *Newsweek* reported a game called Soapies, a new fad for remembering lines, characters, and other trivia from what were already thought of as the good old days of radio soap.

But though the radio soaps are gone, soap opera is not. Today the announcer's voice and the fifteen-minute format are no longer with us, and one does not listen to a favorite soap. Nowadays it's a taped half hour and it's viewed. There are war protesters now, and LSD, and ecology, and other things Mary Noble and Helen Trent had never even heard of. Yet despite all this, the television soaps are clearly an extension of the genre, an adaptation of the primal soap to the audience of today. Just as human nature may be said to be unchanged despite the continual labeling of new generations, counter-cultures, gaps, moralities, and liberations, the soaps too have simply traveled along with us, matching their stride to ours.

Soaps are serials, but not every serial is a soap. Any generalization that can be made about soap opera will have its exceptions, as anyone who has ever followed one knows, but there are general statements that hold true for the form as a whole.

Soap operas are stories about American life. Since most of them are organized around one central family, this means domestic life. The principal characters are white Anglo-Saxon Protestants. They may occasionally have Jewish or Italian names, or come from the wrong side of the tracks, but essentially they fall somewhere near the center on the American graph. Roughly middle-class, not poverty-stricken or, usually, of great wealth, neither ignorant nor well educated, they are people the audience is supposed to be able to identify with. They are generally professional types, doctors, lawyers, psychiatrists, and teachers; money problems rarely afflict them, but the women do their own housework. Manual labor, including domestic help, is in short supply. Asked why so few working-class people appear on soaps, one writer explained that "it's more interesting for a woman to see herself as a doctor's or a lawyer's wife." The people of Soapland, in short, are supposed to be average, just like their audience. As the announcer used to say at the beginning of each episode of radio's *Rosemary,* "This is *your* story—this is *you.*"

But what odd lives these average people live! Blindness,

paralysis, amnesia, and subdural hematoma are as common in Soapland as headaches in everyday life. The women marry again and again. Most of the babies born were fathered by someone other than their mother's husband. People fall in love violently, passionately, often. The Syndicate is taking over. They are being blackmailed by someone who knows their true identity. Above all, they are relentlessly uninhibited conversationalists. There is nothing they will not discuss.

Many aspects of the real world are ignored in Soapland. Work is unimportant, as is religion. No one's life is dedicated to a cause, to political passion, to intellectual curiosity, status, or success. People care little about money, time-killing diversion, or satisfying hobbies. Discard the elements of melodrama, the murder trials, crimes, accidents, and exotic operations, and the subject matter of the soaps is seen to be the emotional relationships of people. These are the relationships of men and women to their children and their parents, but above all to each other.

It is through these relationships that happiness is to be attained, and the deepest belief of everyone in Soapland is that it is indeed attainable by everyone. People in soaps do suffer, as those who disapprove of the serials delight in pointing out, but there are contrasting extremes of joy. A girl in love on a radio soap describes her blissful state of mind to a friend, explaining that "happiness turns a rather drab, rather commonplace, sometimes sad world into the rosiest, most glowing, most shining place . . . It makes people look different. They're not just grumpy and sour—they're to be pitied—and little children—oh, little children have a brand-new meaning. They're so wonderful and exciting. You want to understand them, and listen to them, and laugh with them—because they might be yours—"

Another soap heroine, happily married and a mother after many difficulties, exclaims, "Oh, life does work out so wonderfully, sometimes. If people could just have patience—if they could just get through the hard times and know that around the corner there may be the most glowingly wonderful time waiting for them!"

The central tenet of soap opera is that personal happiness is possible, right here on this earth, for the person who despite all obstacles refuses to despair and continues to strive for it. This happiness is not of a moral sort, not the satisfaction of an end carried out, or a work completed, or a generous decision made with difficulty and steadfastly adhered to; quite the contrary. The vision of supreme happiness that is held out—and demonstrably available to the ordinary, quite average person—is that of happy marriage. Since the goal of everyone's life is happiness—his own, to be sure, not that of others—it is right to strive for it continually.

If the people of Soapland did not hold firmly to that belief, they would have nothing to sustain them as they struggle through their misfortunes. Generally, their determined optimism is rewarded; difficulties do prove transient, the wicked are thwarted, and happiness is at least temporarily assured.

RADIO QUIZ

§

(*Answers on page 24*)

I. Match these radio soaps with their musical themes:

1. *The Story of Mary Marlin*   a. "Juanita"
2. *Lorenzo Jones*   b. "Polly Wolly Doodle"
3. *Backstage Wife*   c. "Red River Valley"
4. *Our Gal Sunday*   d. "Believe Me, If All Those Endear-
                                          ing Young Charms"

5. *The Romance of Helen Trent*   e. "Rose of Tralee"
6. *Aunt Jenny's True Life Stories*   f. "Funiculi, Funicula"
7. *Just Plain Bill*   g. "Clair de Lune"

II. Who invented the three-spouted teapot?

III. Of what profession was each of the following:

1. Joyce Jordan   5. Papa David Solomon
2. Helen Trent   6. Ellen (Young Widder) Brown
3. Mary Marlin   7. Portia (Faces Life) Blake
4. Bess Johnson   8. (Just Plain) Bill Davidson

IV. In the contest to rename David Harum's horse, Xanthippe, which of the 400,000 entries won?

V. Match these soaps with their sponsors:

1. *Life Can Be Beautiful*   a. Oxydol
2. *Ma Perkins*   b. Bab-O
3. *Big Sister*   c. Spry
4. *Aunt Jenny's True Life Stories* d. Old Dutch Cleanser
5. *David Harum*   e. Spic and Span
6. *Bachelor's Children*   f. Rinso

VI. What soap was known in the industry as Elsie Beebe?

VII. Identify the soaps that used these epigraphs:

1. Our years are as the falling leaves . . . we live, we love, we dream . . . and then we go. But somehow we keep hoping, don't we? that our dreams come true on that_____.

2. This is the story of Joan Field—a young girl who came to know that love can be stronger and finer than anything else in the world—perhaps you yourself can remember the thrilling, heartbreaking days that now are hers—and the hopes and dreams and struggles that every young couple experiences before that day of all days . . ._____.

3._____is dedicated to the women of America. The story of a woman who must choose between love and the career of raising other women's children.

4. The story of a brave woman and her brilliant, but unstable husband—the story of her struggle to keep his feet planted firmly on the pathway to success.

5._____. . . the story of a woman who sets out to prove what so many other women long to prove in their own lives . . . that romance can live on at thirty-five . . . and even beyond.

VIII. Match the following soaps with their locale:

1. *Ma Perkins*   a. Five Points
2. *Young Widder Brown*   b. Simpsonville
3. *Big Sister*   c. Stanwood
4. *Vic and Sade*   d. Glens Falls
5. *When a Girl Marries*   e. Elmwood
6. *Pepper Young's Family*   f. Crooper, Illinois
7. *The Guiding Light*   g. Rushville Center

(*Answers on page 24*)

I. Match each pair of siblings in the first column with their family name in the second column and with their soap title in the third column.

a. Leo and Stan	a. Norris	a. *Return to Peyton Place*
b. Rodney and Norman	b. Kurtz	b. *The Edge of Night*
c. Victoria and Meredith	c. Lord	c. *General Hospital*
d. Ken and Holly	d. Harrington	d. *The Guiding Light*
e. Lee and Tom	e. Bauer	e. *One Life to Live*
f. Ed and Michael	f. Pollock	f. *Somerset*
g. Nancy and Cookie	g. Baldwin	

II.

1. Name the actress who has been the leading lady on her serial for more than twenty-two years.

2. Which actress has twice suffered periods of blindness during her tenure as leading lady?

3. Which soap star composes, sings, and accompanies herself on the guitar?

4. Who was the first TV soap star to be nominated for an Emmy award?

III. Which soaps take place in the following locales?

1. Oakdale	a. *The Edge of Night*
2. Springfield	b. *As the World Turns*
3. Monticello	c. *The Secret Storm*
4. Henderson	d. *Another World*
5. Woodbridge	e. *The Guiding Light*
6. Bay City	f. *Search for Tomorrow*
7. Rosehill	g. *Love of Life*
8. Somerset	h. *Somerset*

IV. Which of the following TV soaps do not have a medical doctor as a regular character?

1. *The Young and the Restless*	8. *As the World Turns*
2. *Days of Our Lives*	9. *Return to Peyton Place*
3. *The Doctors*	10. *The Guiding Light*
4. *General Hospital*	11. *The Edge of Night*
5. *One Life to Live*	12. *All My Children*
6. *Search for Tomorrow*	13. *The Secret Storm*
7. *Love of Life*	14. *Somerset*

V.

1. On *Somerset,* Tony is the illegitimate son of _____.

2. On *Search for Tomorrow,* Scott Phillips is the illegitimate son of _____ ; Chris is the illegitimate son of _____.

3. On *Return to Peyton Place*, Allison McKenzie is the illegitimate daughter of _____ and _____.

VI. On *The Guiding Light,* who is Michael Bauer's wife's former brother-in-law?

ANSWERS TO RADIO QUIZ

I. 1-g, 2-f, 3-e, 4-c, 5-a, 6-d, 7-b.
II. Lorenzo Jones. It had one spout for weak tea, one for strong, and one for medium.
III. 1. Doctor. 2. Fashion designer. 3. Senator. 4. Social worker. 5. Proprietor of the Slightly Read Bookshop. 6. Proprietress of a tearoom. 7. Lawyer. 8. Barber.
IV. Town Talk.
V. 1-e, 2-a, 3-f, 4-c, 5-b, 6-d.
VI. *Life Can Be Beautiful* (LCBB).
VII. 1. *The Brighter Day*. 2. *When a Girl Marries*. 3. *Hilltop House*. 4. *Valiant Lady*. 5. *The Romance of Helen Trent*.
VIII. 1-g, 2-b, 3-d, 4-f, 5-c, 6-e, 7-a.

ANSWERS TO TV QUIZ

I. a-bf, b-da, c-ce, d-ad, e-gc, f-ed, g-fb.
II. All Mary Stuart, Joanne Tate of *Search for Tomorrow*.
III. 1-b, 2-e, 3-a, 4-f, 5-c, 6-d, 7-g, 8-h.
IV. None.
V. 1. Laura Cooper.
   2. Doug Martin; Len Whiting.
   3. Constance McKenzie and Elliot Carson.
VI. Michael Bauer. The current Mrs. Michael Bauer was once married to her current brother-in-law, Ed.

BIRTH OF A NOTION

§

Theme: Up and out.

ANNOUNCER: And now . . . *Write to Happiness*, the story of Madeleine, glamorous free-lance writer, and her friend David, versatile actor and onetime suspected child molester, and how, together, they braved the world of soaps, letting no detergent deter them, to reveal the soul and bare the heart of that great American art form—the daytime serial. Our story begins as . . .

We discover Madeleine and David in a tiny office high above Manhattan's sleeping streets. It is late and they are finishing their fourth cup of coffee. Cigarette butts everywhere . . .

MADELEINE: What's wrong, pal?

DAVID: Nothing.

MADELEINE: You can't fool me. You look a little down. I can always tell when something's troubling you.

DAVID: Something is troubling me.

MADELEINE: I knew it.

DAVID: You always know when something is troubling me. You can read me like a book.

MADELEINE: What book?

DAVID [*wryly*]: That's the trouble.

MADELEINE: Yes, the book. But this is the important thing—you've got to keep trying. More coffee?

DAVID: Oh, darn the coffee. We try, don't we, we try! And you're right, we've got to keep on trying. You're right, Mad, you're always right.

MADELEINE [*modestly*]: You're right. So let's keep plugging. Where were we?

DAVID [*despairingly*]: Somewhere this side of *Young Widder Brown* and just rounding into *As the World Turns*. There's no accounting for it.

MADELEINE: What?

DAVID: You know. You always know everything.

MADELEINE: I know. [*Pause. Then valiantly.*] We can only do our best. That's all anyone can do.

DAVID: You're right.

MADELEINE: I know. So let's gird our loins [*Ed. note: This will be cut by air time*] and get down to the business at hand. America is waiting out there. And we're going to give them the best darn book on the soap opera that they've ever dreamed of.

DAVID: I hope you're right, Mad, I hope you're right!

Inconceivable as it may seem, soap opera has not always been with us. In fact, it is not yet fifty years old. There is no real agreement on the exact date of the first soap, since there is no agreement at all on which program should be awarded the title of first soap opera, definitions of the form being appropriately foamy and slippery. Claims and counterclaims, however, are all agreed that the city of the nativity was Chicago (even windier then, perhaps, than now) and that the time was the very late twenties and very early thirties.

The daytime air before soaps was a radio wasteland, and a small one at that. Radio itself had only been in existence in any real sense since 1920, when station KDKA opened up in East Pittsburgh to carry the Harding-Cox election returns. Rapidly it developed into a medium that brought music, sermons, prizefights, and political speeches into the American home; but all that was in the evening. Daytime programing was haphazard, morally uplifting, outrageously dull. There was a program entitled *Mouth Hygiene*, another called *Beautiful Thoughts*. Radio was ready for something new, and gradually the outlines of a new form began to emerge.

James Thurber, in the course of his researches into the world of soap, located an old-time announcer named Norman

Brokenshire, who claimed that he had been the very first in the field, having improvised the daytime serial into existence under the pressure of a programing emergency. Responsible for filling a free half hour of air time with some kind of variety show, he had, he testified, telephoned a number of actors who promised to come up with something. Alas, they were late. After ad-libbing to the limit of his invention, the desperate Brokenshire's gaze fell upon a book lying on a studio table. Mercifully, it turned out to be a collection of short stories, one of which our hero, saved, began to read into the microphone.

Eventually the promised performers made their appearance and took over the remainder of the program, but in the next few days hundreds of disappointed listeners wrote to the studio, begging to hear the end of the story. Brokenshire contended that he had discovered the audience for the as yet uncreated art form, soap opera.

Perhaps he had. But that audience had a long wait ahead before its unconscious thirst could be fully satisfied.

One contender for the first-soap-opera title is a program called *The Smith Family,* first aired in 1925. A young vaudeville couple, Jim and Marion Jordan, happened to be playing Chicago; their agent suggested that a radio program would be valuable publicity. Accordingly, they developed a series, presented one night a week with a repeat on Sunday. Years later Marion Jordan, by then famous as the heroine of *Fibber McGee and Molly,* argued that *The Smith Family* could not be considered soap opera because "the humor was much too broad." But though it was comedy, it certainly contained elements of soap opera. Most important, the characters appeared regularly, so that the audience could get to know them. It was a domestic drama. The central character was a mother whose two nubile daughters were being courted, one by a prizefighter, the other by a Jew.

Another contender, and one that might at first glance seem even more unlikely, also because of its humor, is *Amos 'n' Andy.* Created by Charles Correll and Freeman Gosden, it followed *The Smith Family* by a year, and was indisputably the broadest of comedy. Correll and Gosden had been asked by a Chicago radio station to work up a kind of comic strip of the air, some-thing along the lines of the then popular cartoon strip "The Gumps." Searching their own backgrounds for material they might make use of, they hit upon the idea of Negro life. They explained that they felt qualified to deal with this theme because one of the team had performed in minstrel shows and the other had grown up with a Negro boy his mother had taken into their home.

The show they came up with told the story of two young fellows from Alabama who had decided to seek their fortune in Chicago. One was a sober, industrious youth, willing, and touchingly eager to please; the other was a fast-talking, lazy, crafty, boastful con artist. Their names were Sam and Henry. Sam and Henry came from Birmingham, they belonged to a lodge called Jewels of the Crown, and every day a huge audience tuned in to hear more about the struggle of these two appealing incompetents toward their improbable goals of success, respect-ability, and romance in the big city.

Correll and Gosden, who wrote the scripts and acted all the parts, were such a success that they were soon making records, and within two years they were ready to enlarge the scope of their operation. Unfortunately, the radio station owned the rights to the title *Sam 'n' Henry*. But Correll and Gosden were inventive: they simply changed their characters' names to Amos Jones and Andrew H. Brown. When they changed stations the program was known as *Amos 'n' Andy*, the boys were from Atlanta, and their lodge was the Mystic Knights of the Sea. The audience took these changes in stride, and the show's popularity increased to such an extent that a comic strip based on it was syndicated, and a book of scripts was published.

Clearly Amos and Andy were ready for a nationwide audience, and they were soon to have one. Pepsodent tooth-paste decided to sponsor the show, and NBC was persuaded, albeit with some difficulty, to sell fifteen minutes of radio time six days a week. In those days the traditional units of radio time were hours and half hours, and no other advertiser had tried being on the air so many times a week, so there were misgivings in various quarters.

All those misgivings were apparently justified when the program was first broadcast on August 19, 1929, and the critics scorned it. But the naysayers quickly retreated. The American public knew what it wanted.

Amos 'n' Andy was a fad; it was an addiction; it was a passion and a craze. During its peak years the program was listened to regularly by more than half of all radio-owning families. Telephone use dropped by 50 per cent during the time Correll and Gosden were on the air. The escapades of the boys were known to everyone, and their expressions entered the language. "Um-um, ain't dat sumpin?" and "Don't get me regusted" were everyday speech, and anyone who wasn't spending his days locked in a dark cellar knew who ran the Fresh-Air Taxicab Company of America, Incorpolated. A comic strip made fun of people who proudly announced that they had missed *Amos 'n' Andy* only once: after all, the cartoonist pointed out, this was a boast tens of thousands of people could make. Only the brave souls who postponed their major operations and skipped their daughters' weddings in order to be at the radio instead, never missing a single episode, could qualify as true *Amos 'n' Andy* fans.

It has been said that on a warm summer night it was quite safe for the most dedicated listener to take a walk around the block; the neighbors' open doors and windows would permit him to keep track of every word of his favorite program.

The man in the street wasn't the only one who admired *Amos 'n' Andy*. NBC president Merlin H. Aylesworth said that Correll and Gosden were "working in a new art form" that in many ways resembled the magazine serial and the comic strip and yet was "new and for the air exclusively."

The famous humorist Irvin S. Cobb said: "I claim these two stout fellows won a place in the popular taste and have held it against all comers because they are so natural, so simple, so full of an unforced joyousness, so doggoned human . . . Amos and Andy merely are a couple of genuine, orthodox, true-to-type, flesh-and-blood Afro-Americans who, in their naïve generosity, have extended to me the pleasant boon of being able to listen in on them while they live their lives and have their successes and their failures, their ups and their downs—but more downs than ups."

Today the very title conjures up an ugly vision of racist jokes and vulgar cliché, but Cobb was not alone in thinking of *Amos 'n' Andy* as primarily a story of character. So did its creators. According to Gosden, "Once you establish characters, if they're likable, the public will become fond of them." Correll affectionately described the two principal characters almost as if they were real people. "Amos," he said, "is a hardworking little fellow who tries to do everything he can to help others and to make himself progress, while his friend Andy is not especially fond of hard work and often has Amos assist him in his own duties."

Today the kind of humor that sustained the show would be almost universally offensive, based as it was on racial stereotype, and appealing as it did to the audience's smug assumption of its own infinitely superior sophistication and intelligence. An invitation to self-congratulation was extended to the audience in scene after scene showing the ignorance and ludicrous naïveté of the boys. In this one, they are trying to figure out how much two tickets to Chicago will cost them.

AMOS: Come on—let's sit down yere an' figger dis thing out.

ANDY: Now lissen yere—$26.72—dat's whut it cost each one of us.

AMOS: Now you is got to times dat by two, ain't you?

ANDY: Wait till I do dat yere—twenty-six, seventy-two —times two. Two times two is—a—

AMOS: Dat's four.

ANDY: No, no—two *an'* two is four. We is timesin' yere now.

AMOS: Well, two times two is four, ain't it?

ANDY: Whut we is got do is to mulsify. You is stackin' 'em up, dat's whut you is doin'. Two times two—wait a minute yere now—two times two is six.

AMOS: Two times two is six, huh?

ANDY: An' nothin' to carry—now—a—two times seven—dere's one right dere. We is two timesin' $26.72—two times two is six—nothin' to carry—two times seven.

AMOS: Dat's two sevens, ain't it?

ANDY: Dat can't be seventeen, kin it?

AMOS: I know what dat is. Wait a minute yere—lemme count it on my fingers yere. Dat's fo'teen, ain't it?

ANDY: Dat's whut I jest said. Put down a fo' an' carries one. Now, I'll put dat one up yere by dat six two times sixteen—

AMOS: Whut you goin' do now—mulsify sixteen, huh?

ANDY: Well, I got carry dat one—I puts dat one right in between dat two an' de six.

AMOS: Whut is we mulsifyin'?

ANDY: We'se mulsifyin' $26.72 by two. You see, de fust thing is two times two is six—two times seven is fo'teen—an' I carries one—so dat goes right in between de two an' de six.

AMOS: Dat goes right in between de two an' de six, don't it? Put it dere now an' lemme see how it looks.

ANDY: Wait a minute yere now—I'll put de one in between de two an' de six—dat makes 216 now.

AMOS: Is you goin' mulsify dat 216?

ANDY: Course I goin' mulsify—whut you think I goin' do wid it.

AMOS: Well, whut is dat 216—is dat 216 dollers?

ANDY: You see where I done put dat dot in dere, don't you? Dat makes dat $216.

AMOS: Well, when did we git up in dem big figures?

ANDY: Dat's whut happened when you mulsify.

AMOS: Well, go ahead, do it. You know whut you is doin' dere.

ANDY: Two times 216—lemme see—how much is $216 times two?

AMOS: Well, figgerin' it out in my own haid yere, I figures dat dat's over $400.

ANDY: I b'lieve you is right . . . Dat *is* right—dat's over $400. Two times $26.72, de way I figures yere, is over $400.

AMOS: Dat certainly is a lot o' money fur us to git up dere on, ain't it?

ANDY: Lissen—I got a idea—we'll fool 'em. I'll go one day

an' give $26.72—den de nex' day don' say nothin' to 'em an'
you give $26.72 an' we'll both git dere.

AMOS: Dat's a idea—boy, you certainly do think of 'em.

Yet despite the condescending attitude so clearly invited
by such scenes as this, audiences believed that the Correll-
Gosden approach was essentially sympathetic. The authors
were in great demand as speakers before Negro groups during
the thirties, and have since been widely credited with racial
attitudes far in advance of their times. They have been
applauded for improving understanding between the races by
introducing Negroes for the first time as sympathetic characters
with hopes, dreams, feelings, and family problems the audience
found surprisingly like their own.

Correll and Gosden did include intimate moments in the
lives of their characters, moments that an audience might be
expected to identify with, to some extent at least. The audience
could overhear a father telling a bedtime story to his little girl,
eavesdrop on the last-minute panic of a bridegroom, or listen
in on a painful quarrel between two close friends. In such scenes
as this, the characters and their emotions were meant to be
taken seriously.

ANDY: You kin do de heavy work 'cause you ain't got much
sense as I is, and . . . you is thick-headed.

AMOS: Now, dere you go again, you see. Dat's whut hurts
me, Andy, when you talks to me like dat. I can't help it if
I wuzn't born wid all kind o' brains like big mens is.

ANDY: Now, wait a minute—don't start crying!

AMOS: I know—you tell me not to start cryin'—den you
talk to me like dat—I got feelin's same as you is—how would
you like somebody talkin' to you, tellin' you dey was sumpin'
wrong wid you all de time like dat dat you couldn't help?
Whut kin I do 'bout it?

ANDY: Well, it ain't nothin' you kin do 'bout it, Amos.

AMOS: Well, whut you wants to keep on jumpin' on me
like dat den fur? I tries not to get mad. Ever'thing you done
told me—I listens to it but I'se jest lak a dog or anything else.
You can't keep on beatin' a dog—some day dat dog goin' turn
on you. Down in de dog's heart, he might love you but if

you keep on beatin' him an' he loves you jest de same—but he goin' turn on you.

ANDY: I ain't beatin' you—I ain't tryin' to beat you.

AMOS: No, you ain't beatin' me wid yore fist—you ain't tryin' to beat me wid yore fist—but you'se beatin' at my heart —dat's whut you'se beatin' at. Dat's de worst kin' o' beatin' anybody kin take too.

ANDY: Don't feel dat way, Amos. Let's furgit it.

AMOS: It's easy enough fur you to tell me not to feel dat way but when somebody's always cuttin' you like dey's cuttin' you wid a knife—hurtin' yore feelin's an' hurtin' yore pride an' ever'thing else, it ain't so easy to say—"let's furgit it."

ANDY: Ain't I yore buddy?

AMOS: You is my buddy a'right, Andy, an' I is yore buddy too, I hopes. Dat's why I can't understan' sometime de way you jump on me. Sometime I think dat if you did love me down in yore heart, you wouldn't talk to me de way you do.

ANDY: Amos, ev'vy time I talk to you like dat, it's fur yore own good.

AMOS: I knows you tries to do things fur me—I knows you try to help me. I b'lieve you'd do anything in de world fur me if it come right down to it. I don't care whut anybody say, I b'lieve if someboddy bigger dan I wuz jumped on me, I b'lieve you'd jump in dere an' help me if it killed you—an' I'd do de same thing fur you, Andy—but please don't talk 'bout me no mo' dat hurts my feelin's, will you?

ANDY: Well, you knows I'se sorry if I hurt yore feelin's.

AMOS: Don't think dat I'se a big baby 'cause I'se standin' yere wid tears in my eyes. Nobody'll ever know how I feel till dey feels like I do.

ANDY: Come on—put on yore hat—let's go out an' git some fresh air.

AMOS: I don't care—I'll walk around wid you an' git a little fresh air. But don't be mad wid me now 'cause I said dat—I jest had to git it off my chest, dat's all.

ANDY: Come on—we'll go down an' see a movin' pitcher show or sumpin'—dat'll make you feel better—put yore arm around me.

AMOS: I'se wid you—come on.

Amos 'n' Andy was certainly not a true soap, but mixed into its heavy-handed treatment of stock comedy situations were many of the main elements that would soon be defined as soap opera. First, and most important, it was a serial. In addition, there were central characters with whom the listener could at least occasionally identify, whose ups and downs he could follow, with whom he could establish something very like a friendship; for these were, by and large, likable characters. And though episodes were self-contained, there was the kind of general suspense, based on audience curiosity about and interest in what will happen to the characters, that is part of soap opera to this day.

It was only to be expected that the huge success of *Amos 'n' Andy* would inspire imitation. Pepsodent was selling as never before, and other advertisers hoped for similar results with similar programs. Within two years of the program's arrival in the big time, it had more than a dozen competitors.

The protagonists of these shows were not black, but many of the writers tried to stake out an ethnic claim of their own, just as Correll and Gosden had. Picturesque Down Easters, hillbillies, and immigrants jostled each other for air time, their dialects frequently approaching authentic incomprehensibility.

Lum and Abner, one of the most successful of these programs, was primarily a comedy with few soap elements. The action unfolded in the mythical village of Pine Ridge, Arkansas, where life centered around the Jot 'Em Down Store. Such characters as Lum Edwards, Grandpappy Spears, Cedric Weehunt and Snake Hogan, Doc Miller, Squire Skimp and Dick Huddleston proved so attractive to their listeners that the town of Waters, Arkansas, decided to change its name to Pine Ridge in their honor.

But *Moonshine and Honeysuckle,* another folksy serial based on the lives of Southern mountain people, though aired only once a week, approached very closely what soap opera would eventually be. True, dialect was thick, and there was more of the familiar *Amos 'n' Andy* style of humor, based on an appeal to supposed audience superiority. In a humorous scene Pink

Freeze receives a letter; his friend Clem helps him to read and reply to it.

PINK: Clem, I've got a letter. I've got a letter.

CLEM: Who from?

PINK: Durned if I know. Maybe somebody's dead.

CLEM: Why don't ye read hit?

PINK: I would, but—er—I ain't seen my specks fer two or three years and I don't exactly know whar to lay my hands on 'em.

CLEM: Want me to read hit, Pink?

PINK: If hit ain't no trouble.

CLEM: None, if the writin's plain.

PINK: Here, I've got hit opened and everything.

CLEM: Supposin' hit's private?

PINK: Private?

CLEM [*teasingly*]: From a girl or something.

PINK: Oh! Well, if hit's very private don't read hit.

CLEM: Won't know till I read hit, Pink.

PINK: Couldn't ye read jest a little bit out loud?

CLEM: Hit's printed like a book.

PINK: Must be mighty important.

CLEM: We'll see. [*Reads.*] Thar's yo' name and town and hit says: Dear Mr. Freeze: Air ye i-n-t-e-r-interested in im-p-r-o-v-improvin' yo' c-o-n-d-i-tion condition?

PINK: Ain't that nice of him?

CLEM: If so, fill out the enclosed blank and send hit with ten cents in stamp and we will mail ye i-n-s-t-r-u-c-t-i-o-n-s.

PINK: Whut's that?

CLEM: I don't know. Something he wants to send ye. Patent medicine, maybe.

PINK: Well, I declare. Is that all?

CLEM: 'Bout. Hopin' to hear, etc.

PINK: Well, who in the world is he?

CLEM: Hit says Ideal Improvement Co.

PINK: I cain't recollect him. Kin ye?

The two mountaineers laboriously begin to answer the letter. "Dear Mr. Co," Pink dictates. "Yo' welcome letter to hand. I take my pen in hand to say I positively don't know ye. My memory is bad for names." But then the solution comes to him. "Oh, yes," he exclaims, "I just recollect a man named Co that run away with my wife's sister!"

He resumes his dictation: "I knowed a man that run away with my wife's sister. If ye air him, and ain't dead, lemme know how ye all air. Ye kin say I'm well. Tell him poor Ella ain't no more. Mention that my baby can near 'bout talk. And to excuse writin', spellin' and words left out. Give my love to his wife. And say nothin' 'bout the ten cents." "Till ye git better acquainted," Clem qualifies.

An audience that enjoyed Andy's expert mulsifying could be expected to find this demonstration of ineptitude equally amusing, yet *Moonshine and Honeysuckle* was far closer to real soap opera than *Amos 'n' Andy.* The main characters, whatever their lacks in education and polish, are unquestionably meant to be taken seriously. Their emotions are given full weight, their setting, Lonesome Hollow, is described as beautiful, and they themselves are attractive people. The announcer sets the scene, introducing the hero, Clem Betts: "This unearthly beauty, a ghostly stir and murmur among the leaves, and the soft air burdened with honeysuckle, play upon Clem's romantic senses. A vague heartbreaking loneliness haunts him. In spirit, he is a potential lover and poet." When Clem falls in love, his feelings are not made in the least ludicrous or contemptible; he is an acceptable romantic hero, and the girl he loves is another appealing and attractive character.

The Goldbergs, which was to become the best known and most durable of all the ethnic soaps, made frequent use of humorous ethnic stereotype and the appeal to snobbery, but it placed its main reliance on human, likable characters. As a spokesman for the network described the author's intentions in the program's early days: "Miss Berg . . . has shown herself to be a preacher of the bright side of life despite some of life's sordidness. She has revealed her passion for the love of friendship, and her fervent belief that every cloud has a silver lining. She has endeavored to point out that pecuniary success is not justifiable except insofar as it is employed as a means to aid the moral and spiritual progress of one's fellowmen."

Molly Goldberg, the show's central character, boasts about her children in stereotypical and malapropistic fashion. "Mrs. Bloom vould only vish," she says to her husband, "to have soch two children like ve got. Sammy is also a diamond! From school to *cheder*—from *cheder* to home—and from home to wiolin. I'm telling you, Jake, he's growing op a Mischa Heifetz! Come, listen, how he plays his new piece and Rosie plays the accomplishment."

But despite her comic failings, Molly is meant to be taken very seriously as mother and woman. Family feeling runs deep. When Molly asks her daughter, "You'll vouldn't be ashamed from your mama, ha, Rosielie?" the child responds, "Ashamed of you, Mama? I'm so proud of you if I had a whole world of mamas to choose from I'd pick you!"

Husband Jake appreciates her too. When Molly accuses him, "You're laughing from me, ha?" he is quick to disavow any such intention. "God forbid I should laugh from you, Molly! It vould be a fine day I should laugh from you! If it vasn't far you, vould dere be a Molly Cloik und Soot Company? I'll never forget dat night I came home so disgusted, and you handled me over de monneh from de blue pitcher to start in beezness. Ah, Molly, a man ain't a voman! A man don't talk much, but de more he's got in de heart de less his tongue vaggles. Molly, mine dear, tings is coming along better even dan I expected."

Gertrude Berg, creator of *The Goldbergs,* played the part of Molly herself. When she first tried to sell her sketches of Lower East Side life to NBC in 1929, so the story goes, they were written in so impenetrable a longhand that she was forced to read them aloud, thus unwittingly auditioning for the lead. The network, having launched *Amos 'n' Andy* only three months before, felt it was taking a chance on this somewhat unorthodox and thoroughly unproved amateur, but its faith was justified by a twenty-year success.

Unquestionably, *The Goldbergs* was a soap. Comedy there was, but the series reflected a quintessential domesticity, presided over by a powerful and benevolent woman; its subject matter was human relations, and its surface was resolutely realistic. Mrs. Berg, in fact, was so dedicated to authenticity that she made periodic trips to the Lower East Side, to steep herself anew in the milieu from which her scripts had sprung. The eggs the Goldbergs' audience heard sizzling in the pan were being fried right there in the studio. When Sammy Goldberg went off to join the Army, the family farewells were actually said in Grand Central Station.

The Goldbergs ran happily on until 1945, when it was dropped by its sponsor. After World War II the family, now suburbanites, made a brief, unsatisfactory comeback on television.

One more contender for the "first" crown must be mentioned, *Clara, Lu 'n' Em.* Its claim is not based so much on its central nature as on the fact that it was the first daytime serial on network radio. Other shows were closer to what soaps would eventually be, but they were aired at night, or were weekly rather than daily, or belonged to local radio stations. *Clara, Lu 'n' Em* has its small, undisputed distinction.

As was often the case in the early days of radio, the writers of this program played the parts they wrote. The show had been improvised by three friends, Louise Starkey (Clara), Isobel Carothers (Lu), and Helen King (Em), while they were students together at Northwestern. Their sorority sisters so much enjoyed their performances that they were emboldened to take their creation to a Chicago radio station, which put the program on the air in 1930. From there as a nighttime show it leaped to national status and daytime air, establishing the fifteen-minute, five-day-a-week pattern later adopted by all the radio soaps.

By nature the show was a gentle comedy, but it was certainly domestic, woman-oriented, and dealt mainly with personal relationships. The leading character was Em, harried mother of five and a neglected wife. Clara was her housekeeper, and Lu the widow who lived in the upstairs duplex. In the beginning the three young authors simply outlined the basic situation to be dealt with the following day and then improvised on the air; as time passed, they produced more formal scripts. Their method of composition suggests that they avoided strong dramatic action in favor of commentary, with the characters more observers than participants.

Clara, Lu 'n' Em was successful until 1936; then, suddenly, Isobel Carothers (Lu) died. Rather than substitute another actress in the role, the two remaining friends took the program off the air. When they tried to revive it six years later with another friend playing the part of Lu, they found they had lost their audience, presumably to newer, more exciting soaps.

During this transitional period, before the real heyday of the soaps, another, very different kind of daytime serial made its debut in 1932. This was Paul Rhymer's *Vic and Sade,* described by *Time* magazine in 1943 as the best soap opera on the air. The program, however, had very little in common with real soap opera. True, it was a daily serial, with continuing characters. It was on daytime air, fifteen minutes a day, five days a week. And it certainly dealt with domestic matters. Rhymer claimed that he was writing a program about family life, drawing upon his memories of the people among whom he grew up in Bloomington, Indiana. Sade was supposedly inspired by Rhymer's mother.

But this description is decidedly misleading. It does not even remotely suggest the true nature of *Vic and Sade,* or the vast gulf that separates it from soap opera. In the first place, it was funny. Other shows with distinctly soaplike elements had been primarily comic, but those programs had an emotional subtext *Vic and Sade* laid no claim to. Characters on these borderline shows gave clear indications that beneath their amusing or stereotypical or clownish or impenetrably ethnic exteriors, there was deep human feeling. Vic and Sade had no feelings. Surface was all, and that surface represented a comic distortion of everyday life. This makes *Vic and Sade* almost an inversion of true soap opera.

In a true soap, a realistic background is essential. If the breakfast eggs sizzle authentically in their pan, the audience will more willingly believe the subsequent breakfast conversation, no matter how improbable. If the characters inhabit a small, average town where they own a Cape Cod cottage, mow their lawns, and drink endless cups of coffee even as does the audience, then it is easier for that audience to establish a connection with the characters and to believe that their emotions are genuine, their tears wet, and their problems worth solving. The seamless realistic surface exists to convince the audience that it is somehow privileged to eavesdrop not on an evanescent theatrical performance but on life itself, the real subterranean life of those other people who share our world but conceal their truths from us.

But nobody was ever intended to establish an emotional bond with Vic and Sade. Nobody could possibly identify with them. Their world is plainly skewed from the start. Victor Rodney Gook, chief accountant of the Consolidated Kitchenware Company, Plant No. 14, lives with his wife Sade and their adopted twelve-year-old son Rush Meadows, in "the small house halfway up in the next block" in Crooper, Illinois. Their friends, most of whom never appear, are such personages as L. Vogel Drum, Botch Purney, that attractive divorcée Cora Bucksaddle, the Reverend Kidneyslide, Gus Plink, and, of course, Rishigan Fishigan (of Shishigan, Michigan).

These people have their idiosyncrasies. Mr. Buller, head of Consolidated Kitchenware, pulls his own teeth. Godfrey Dimlok has invented a bicycle that can say "Mama." Rush has a dog, Mr. Albert Johnson, who is astigmatic and cannot bark. Sade spends a lot of her spare time chatting on the phone with her dearest friend Ruthie Stembottom, planning a shopping expedition downtown for a washcloth sale, or a get-together at the Petite Pheasant Feather Tea Shoppe. At the end of the show, the announcer might give a credit: "Sade's gowns by Yamelton's Department Store, Crooper, Illinois."

In a typical episode, Vic and Sade discuss from every angle Sade's Uncle Fletcher's choice of a birthday gift for his landlady, a four-foot length of railway track that weighs 440 pounds and would, Uncle Fletcher suggests, make a wonderful doorstop. This kind of thing went on for thirteen years, ending only when Rhymer decided to lay down his pen, but all of it was a million miles from soap opera.

The success of *Vic and Sade* does suggest another route the daytime serial might have traveled, into comedy, fantasy, parody, satire, and a variety of private visions, but that was not what happened. All the elements that would become soap opera had now made their appearance; they had only to be combined and offered to an audience that was waiting eagerly for a new invention in entertainment, something they could not have defined but that they would immediately recognize as their own.

DAVID: I can't go on.

MADELEINE: You've got to.

DAVID: I know, but . . . [*faltering*]

MADELEINE: Go on.

DAVID [*Lifting his head wearily off the typewriter keys*]: Why, Mad, I never noticed before . . . that sure is a purty pin you're wearing there.

MADELEINE: I know, it is lovely, isn't it? Can you see the seven imitation-ruby, glass-colored, gemlike beads set in the platinum-tinted, chrome-based, gold-filled, heart-shaped plastic?

DAVID: I am dazzled by its subtle beauty.

MADELEINE: If you look at it just so, it says "Madeleine" and this way it says "Mother."

DAVID: And on the back it says "twenty-five cents."

MADELEINE: Yes, I wanted to tell my friends that with just one quarter and three inside labels from my family-size sponsor, they too can have a "Mad-Mother" pin. Allow six weeks for delivery.

DAVID: You sound like an early radio soap opera heroine.

MADELEINE: That's because I'm generous, warmhearted, intuitively bright, and rather meddlesome.

DAVID: Right again, Mad.

All the elements of soap were now present, soon to coalesce into one instantly recognizable form. And Soapland was soon to be divided into three parts, ruled by the three most famous names in soap history: Irna Phillips, Elaine Carrington, and the Hummerts. They all wheeled into view on the soap horizon at the same time. Although their personalities differed, they shared some central beliefs about storytelling, what the world was like, and what audiences were waiting for.

Not only did they dominate the field; they dominated it to such an extent that they determined and defined what soap opera unalterably became. They took what had gone before and selected from it the elements they wanted. They invented a stock of plot devices, characterizations, and storytelling methods. And of course for the next twenty years they influenced and reinfluenced each other.

At the start, nobody could have predicted it. Irna Phillips, for example, must have seemed an average young woman— brown-haired, blue-eyed, bright, and energetic, but surely not marked by destiny. She had a job teaching storytelling and children's theater when, at the age of twenty-eight, her life reached an accidental turning point.

In 1930, while on a visit to her native Chicago, she took a tour of the broadcasting studios. A confused director thought she had come to audition as an actress and shoved a book into her hands. So impressive was her reading of Eugene Field's poem "The Bow-leg Boy" that she was immediately offered a job. The job was unpaid, and she refused it, but no doubt she felt this proved something about her affinity for radio, and it was not long before she returned to Chicago and accepted the unpaid assignment of writing and performing a half-hour show. She followed that up with an entire summer of unpaid radio work. Only then, on the verge of departure for another winter of teaching, was she at last offered a real paying job.

It is tempting to speculate about how different the history of radio—and later television—might have been if Irna Phillips had been asked to turn out an improvisational children's fairy tale series, a group of science documentaries, or an educational interview program. Fortunately for the future of soap opera, she was not. Station WGN offered her fifty dollars a week to write a "family serial" to be called *Painted Dreams*.

Painted Dreams was not the first soap opera, but it established

Irna Phillips immediately in the mainstream of suds. From its beginning in 1932 it had everything to qualify it as a soap. It told the story of kindly old Mother Moynihan, her grown children, and their friends. Essentially it was domestic and woman-oriented and dealt with personal relationships. The connecting lives of the various characters provided a variety of intertwined plot lines, some slowly developing as others receded or were resolved. And the message was that marriage, love, and motherhood were, whatever anyone might argue, woman's highest destiny and fulfillment.

Irna Phillips did not seek her own destiny and fulfillment in family life, however. She was beginning to have a quite different sense of her own direction in life, and suggested to WGN that *Painted Dreams* should be sold to a network, to the greater fulfillment of everybody's destiny. When the station refused, she went to court. Unfortunately, the decision went against her: though she had copyrighted a number of her scripts, it was held that since the station had originated the idea and title for the show, it remained their property.

Nothing daunted, Irna Phillips solved her problem just as Gosden and Correll had solved theirs a few years earlier. She simply changed the name of her show, assigned aliases to all her characters, and proceeded on her upward path. Mother Moynihan became Mother Moran, *Painted Dreams* was converted to *Today's Children,* and the "new" show was soon a great success on NBC.

The message of *Today's Children* was that of *Painted Dreams*: marriage is a woman's finest career. When Frances, the elder daughter and an aspiring artist, complained that she did not see why a wedding ring should interfere with "the realization of the dream that I've been painting almost all my life," Mother Moran replied: "Frances, you are paintin' your dreams, yes. And you hold the brush and must be choosin' the colors to use. But when you're paintin' your dreams, be careful of the colors you're goin' to be usin', 'cause sometimes you make a mistake, and the colors that you think are goin' to look good don't look so good in the finished picture. Now, Frances, darlin', let me be sayin' just one more thing to ya. There are three colors that have stood the test of all time. They are the colors that are the foundation of all dreams of all the men and women in the world—the colors of love . . . family . . . home.''

Mother Moran explained her principles to a feminist this way: ''In your plan, women wouldn't be havin' time to be havin' children and keepin' a home . . . I'm thinkin' that a country is only as strong as its weakest home. When you're after destroyin' those things which make up a home, you're destroyin' people.''

Irna Phillips was a shrewd businesswoman, and she learned her lesson from the loss of *Painted Dreams.* From that time forth, she was careful to establish her rights to any material she originated, and that was to be a great deal of material. *Woman in White, Right to Happiness, The Guiding Light, Road of Life, Lonely Women*—all vastly successful. By the mid-thirties she was making a quarter of a million dollars a year.

Miss Phillips started out typing her own scripts. According to legend, her race against the clock was often so dramatic that pages were mimeographed just as they fell from her typewriter and handed directly to the actors without editing. Then she learned to dictate her scripts to a stenographer, either sitting on the arm of a chair or pacing up and down as she acted out all the parts. During this phase she allegedly churned out 60,000 words a week, which is a good three million words a year.

All this has a dubious ring. In view of the fact that the public likes its superhumans to stay on their pedestals, perhaps it should be allowed to pass, but one greets with relief the later, more sober announcement that Miss Phillips had bowed to the human condition to the extent of hiring a group of assistants.

To say that she used assistant writers, however, is in no way meant to take away any credit for her superb inventiveness, her vast energy, and her unwaveringly clear sense of the emotional center of the audience mind. She was a powerful creative force, and soap opera bore her imprint from the beginning.

What's more, it still does. Irna Phillips is still active in television. And though there were others who loomed as large as she in radio soap days, it is safe to say that she is the single most important influence on television soaps. Not only has she originated some of the most successful and most copied shows, but she is called in as a consultant when ratings dip or new writers need guidance.

The second writing soaperstar was Elaine Carrington. She came to radio not, like Irna Phillips, as an unpaid amateur but as an established writer of women's-magazine fiction. One day, caught in a rainstorm, she took refuge in a nearby radio station. She had some short stories in her purse and, using her time constructively, decided to try to sell them. Impressed by her work, the radio people asked her to think of an idea for a daytime serial. Elaine Carrington hardly knew what they were talking about.

Her first venture into radio was a weekly half hour called *Red Adams,* and its debut was noted in 1932 by *The New York Times*: "RED ADAMS APPEARS—Elaine Sterne Carrington, whose stories have hitherto found their way between magazine covers and into celluloid, now turns to a new medium, the microphone. Beginning tomorrow, her sketch, *Red Adams,* will be presented for WJZ's audience at 10:30 P.M."

Red Adams was the story of a supposedly typical, happy-go-lucky, middle-class teen-ager, who lived in the supposedly typical small town of Oak Park with his mother, father, and younger sister. Red closely resembled Willie of Booth Tarkington's *Seventeen,* just as Andy Hardy would later resemble him.

Sometimes Red's father failed to understand his deep need to borrow the family car, but his mother was unfailingly, if humorously, sympathetic, and Dad always eventually came around. Little sister was bratty, nosy, but always, ultimately, worshipful. The mysterious allure of the opposite sex fueled most plot developments. Red spent his time falling in and out of love with visiting actresses and other exotic out-of-towners, usually a good bit older than he or in some other way unsuitable. His sighs, and presumably his feelings, were deep but never lasting. The most serious result of heartbreak would be a week or two of misogynistic planning with the fellows to form an all-male club and retire to permanent rural bachelorhood.

Irna Phillips, doyenne of soap writers for forty years and still going.

Paul Rhymer, author of *Vic and Sade,* won many trophies and citations.

Anne Hummert created dozens of soaps with her husband, Frank.

Elaine Carrington posed in 1943 to celebrate Episode No. 500 of *When a Girl Marries*.

All this was appealing enough to entice a sponsor, Beech-Nut Gum. Since the other big name in the chewing-gum field at the time was Adams, Red's name had to be changed to Red Davis. The show was now aired three times a week, but otherwise Red was pretty much the same boy. A few years later, when Procter & Gamble took over Red and his family, the program's name was changed again, this time to *Forever Young.* The central character was renamed Pepper Young; the color of his hair remained constant, even though there were certain alterations in the family circle. The Youngs weren't quite as prosperous as the Adamses had been. There was less talk of a future for their boy at Yale. There was no longer a room in the house known as the library. Their hometown was Elmwood now. But essentially they were the same family, and they were to remain so, five days a week, for many years, reaching their final designation as *Pepper Young's Family.*

Pepper's teen years could not be prolonged indefinitely, and eventually he grew up, married, and became mayor of Elmwood. The plots, influenced over the years by other soaps, lost some of their nostalgic flavor and matured with the characters. The world, that is to say, became a more serious place, and the show that had started out with many comic elements settled into middle age as a full-fledged soap.

Mrs. Carrington was prospering. The success of *Pepper Young's Family* was so phenomenal, in fact, that in 1938 it was being carried by both NBC and CBS, and was being presented at three different hours every day. Mrs. Carrington branched out, creating several other programs, including *Rosemary, When a Girl Marries,* and *Marriage for Two. When a Girl Marries* was to last for eighteen years, and had perhaps the largest audience among the radio soaps.

Within fifteen years Mrs. Carrington's radio income had vaulted from the seventy-five dollars a week she had earned from *Red Adams* to about $4500 a week, or $234,000 a year.

By 1938 Mrs. Carrington was reportedly writing 38,000 words each week, not precisely threatening Irna Phillips's record 60,000 but certainly creeping up. Perhaps Mrs. Carrington was not quite as superhumanly prolific as Miss Phillips, but she, too, was supposed to be capable of dictating all those words, dramatically and unaided, to a machine. She was said to do this in various ways: "standing usually," said Thurber; "lying down," said Max Wylie; "lying on a couch," said her son Robert; "plopped down on a seven-foot bed," said the writer of the *Times* obituary in 1958. Mrs. Carrington was reported to achieve all this between the hours of ten and four each day, with plenty of time out in the middle for a leisurely lunch, and this during a period when she was writing three different shows.

Mrs. Carrington never listened to a playback of her dictation. Indeed, she rarely listened to one of her own broadcasts, and said she had never listened even once to any other soap opera. However, she was a frequent guest at rehearsals, where she defended her dialogue with great resolution against any suggested cuts or changes. Her famous romantic scenes, on which she prided herself, often included such flights as "I'd like to give you the whole world as a bauble to swing at your wrist," and the powerful authoress was adamant in her insistence that this flavor be preserved. Here's a snatch of a typical Carrington love scene:

BILL: I love you, Rosemary, the way—the way a man loves life—the way he feels when he's on a battlefield and men are dead all around him and he's unhurt and takes great gulps of air into his lungs and sobs "I'm alive!"—that's how I love you—

ROSEMARY: Oh, Bill—

BILL: I love you the way a man loves—loves his home, and the sky at night full of stars, and a fire on the hearth—the way he loves the ocean and the way he loves mountains and the way he loves little quiet places under the trees—

ROSEMARY: Bill! . . . Bill!

BILL: My darling . . . my love . . . my precious . . .

[*Sound of kiss.*]

ROSEMARY: I love you that way, too, Bill—it doesn't make sense. I haven't known you long. I don't know what you're really like, but I love you—with—with all I've got to love a man with—all of me—every ounce—

Whatever the literary merits of such dialogue, it brought

Mrs. Carrington not only riches but fame as well. Most radio writers were anonymous, but before and after every Carrington show, her name was clearly announced. The announcer might say: "Procter & Gamble White Laundry Soap—for cleaner, whiter clothes—brings you—*Rosemary!*" After a two-second pause he would continue: "*Rosemary*—written by Elaine Carrington, author of *Pepper Young's Family* and *When a Girl Marries*—is dedicated to all the women of today."

While *Pepper Young's Family* changed a good deal over its lifetime, Mrs. Carrington's other radio shows did not. They began and continued as soaps. Only one, *Marriage for Two,* was short-lived. Mrs. Carrington often used humor in her writing; she frequently introduced youthful characters, complete with current slang. She was able to invent, change, improvise, and insouciantly put almost anything behind her. These qualities charmed, infuriated, or intimidated everyone she worked with. Her temperament exactly suited her slapdash art, and she thoroughly enjoyed life in her New York penthouse and Bridgehampton summer place (which she referred to as "the house Camay built"). So relaxed was her approach that she is said to have appeared on at least one gala occasion decked out in lace evening gown and canvas oxfords. Unfortunately, she did not live long enough to stamp her influence on television; her only TV program, *Follow Your Heart,* lasted only three months.

Yet gifted and innovative as Irna Phillips and Elaine Carrington unquestionably were, they were not as influential in setting the pattern of soap opera as the two people who during the thirties and forties seemed on the verge of monopolizing the field, Frank and Anne Hummert.

Facts about the Hummerts are hard to come by. Frank's birth date is not known. Supposedly he was a Texas Ranger for two years, after which he put in a stint at the St. Louis *Post-Dispatch*. He seems to have knocked around rewriting plays and managing a writing school before entering the advertising business, where at last he found himself, originating a World War I slogan that was much admired, at least in advertising circles: BONDS OR BONDAGE. His main contribution to the art of advertising was the idea that ads could be written as if they were feature news. The idea caught on; his name was made. From advertising he went on to produce radio programs. Eventually, he was lured from New York to Chicago by an agency that encouraged him to build up his own radio production unit.

Hummert was resolutely opposed to having women work in his office, but one day, just as it might have happened in a soap, a young woman appeared in search of a job. She was small, attractive, smartly dressed; she was married to a man she had met while working as a reporter—or, some people say, writer of an advice to the lovelorn column—on the Paris *Herald,* and she was the mother of a young son. Like any soap opera hero in such a situation, Hummert resisted the idea of hiring her as his assistant, but was eventually prevailed upon to give her a chance. The rest, one might say, is herstory.

Anne Ashenhurst (the small, smartly dressed young woman) and Hummert formed their own production company in New York, and started to take over the soap opera. In 1935 they married and set up housekeeping in Connecticut.

Think of a famous soap opera title, and chances are you're thinking of a Hummert property. *Amanda of Honeymoon Hill, Backstage Wife, David Harum, Front Page Farrell, John's Other Wife, Just Plain Bill, Lorenzo Jones, Nona from Nowhere, Our Gal Sunday, The Romance of Helen Trent, Stella Dallas, Young Widder Brown, Betty and Bob.* And more.

Frank Hummert has sometimes been given credit for originating the idea of the soap opera. Though this is not strictly true, it is true that he had *an* idea of the form. Of course others were inventing soap opera at the same time, but when he and his young assistant, Mrs. Ashenhurst, started to concern themselves with serials, they brought to bear such a combination of common sense, advertising know-how, production expertise, and just plain efficiency that they made the form their own and would eventually, to a greater extent than anyone else, set their stamp upon it.

The Hummerts explained their serials as "successful stories about unsuccessful people." By "unsuccessful" they meant only that their characters were not rich. In other than a material sense, they were by no means failures. "They may be very successful in their family life," Hummert pointed out in an interview, "or in the way they manage to help their neighbors and their friends. Our stories are about the everyday doings of plain, everyday people—stories that can be understood and appreciated on Park Avenue and on the prairie."

Many of their soaps were founded upon a social gap. *Our Gal Sunday,* in what has become the most famous cliché of old-time radio, announced itself as "the story of an orphan girl named Sunday, from the little mining town of Silver Creek, Colorado, who in young womanhood married England's richest, most handsome lord, Lord Henry Brinthrope. The story asks the question, Can this girl from a mining town in the West find happiness as the wife of a wealthy and titled Englishman?"

Backstage Wife was another story of a simple girl, this time an Iowa stenographer, who marries above her station. The program told "what it means to be the wife of a famous Broadway star—dream sweetheart of a million other women."

Stella Dallas was founded on a veritable social chasm. It was "a continuation on the air of the true-to-life story of mother love and sacrifice, in which Stella Dallas saw her own beloved daughter Laurel marry into wealth and society and, realizing the differences in their tastes and worlds, went out of Laurel's life."

As for Bill Davidson, eponymous hero of *Just Plain Bill,* Mrs. Hummert explained his appeal in the only speech she is known to have made. "So," she said, "we put this man of the Middle West—the fact that he was from the Middle West makes him a great favorite; people seem to like characters from that section best—in this situation. Here he was talking to his assistant: 'My daughter is coming home today. I haven't seen her in eighteen years. She's been East with her aunt, in fine finishing schools, and doesn't even know I'm her father. Is she going to be too good for me?' "

As Frank Hummert summed up the basic question of the show in an interview, the problem was, "Will she look down on her pa or will she accept him and adjust herself to his simple mode of living?"

The Hummerts' own story did not deal with unsuccessful people. Indeed, it was the archetypical American success story. Within a few years of their meeting, they were running a large and enormously profitable mass-production manufacturing operation. By 1938 they were buying one eighth of all radio time at a cost of $12 million a year, and they were responsible for 6.5 million yearly words. Their factory was organized as a rigid hierarchy. At the top were the Hummerts themselves. Laboring on the lower rungs were approximately twenty writers, six script readers or editors, and some sixty clerical assistants.

Secluding themselves in their Greenwich home, the Hummerts themselves created the title and a rough summary of the theme of each show. When this reached the office, it was put into shape, emerging as four or five pages of double-spaced typewriting. Next the Hummerts would create the story line, a sketch of the action to take place during the next five or six episodes. The story line occupied about four double-spaced pages. Then the statement of the theme, along with the story line, would be sent to five writers. All these writers produced sample scripts, and the writer of the best samples got the job. From then on, he or she was supposed to stay three weeks ahead at all times. One of the six script readers was assigned to keep in touch, relaying to the writer whatever new inspirations of character and plot might occur to the Hummerts, or any dissatisfaction that might cross their minds. All communication between employees and headquarters was in writing. As a network executive remarked at the time, "The operation works just like General Motors." There were inevitable comparisons between the Hummert word factory and the workshop in which Alexandre Dumas turned out his 277 volumes with the assistance of some sixty anonymous apprentices.

The Hummerts were feared and their whims were all-powerful. One dialoguer who had managed to get himself nineteen scripts ahead so he could take a trip to Mexico was suddenly informed that Mrs. Hummert wanted to change the plot; vacation plans abandoned, he got back to the typewriter. Hummert hirelings were expected to toil relentlessly and with few incentives. They were not even well paid, and top executives in the organization might receive a box of cookies as their Christmas gift.

Yet they all labored on, and with remarkable success. Perhaps the system engendered a pleasurable feeling of security among the workers. There was a rule or set of rules laid down by the Hummerts to govern almost any contingency. Directors were forbidden to introduce any artistic effects, such as background music or sound not absolutely dictated by the script, that might interfere with the clarity of the dialogue. The actors, the Hummerts insisted, must have the clearest possible enunciation, so that not one precious syllable might elude the listener. There was to be no overlapping of speeches.

Writers had their own regulations to abide by. Every character must be clearly identified at all times. Every detail of the plot must be explained, clearly enough for every member of the audience, even the slowest, to grasp, and often enough to permit the negligent listener to catch up with missed plot developments. Under these conditions, characterization could hardly be subtle. There must never be a doubt in the audience's mind as to what was going on, why, when, where, and whose fault it all was.

All this careful work was done in the name of the housewife. The typical fan was assumed to be trotting about her daily chores with mop in one hand, duster in the other, cooking, tending babies, answering telephones. Thus occupied, she might not be able to bring her full powers of concentration to bear on *Backstage Wife*. So *Backstage Wife* had to be powerful enough to hold her interest despite all interruptions and bring her back for more.

Soap opera scripts were usually mimeographed in black, and the cover page offered the title, the author's name, and the cast list. Not so a Hummert script. The usual title-page information appeared in lavender ink, as did the fact that this script was a "Hummert Radio Feature," that the "authors of title and original story line" were Frank and Anne Hummert, and that the "general supervisors of script and production" were Frank and Anne Hummert. Moreover, the lavender message continued, "this unpublished drama or radio adaptation is the property of Frank and Anne Hummert and is being used under special license to Air Features, Inc. . . . It is fully protected under common law copyright law. Damages will be demanded for unauthorized performances thereof or for the making of unauthorized copies thereof either for publication, radio, or motion pictures. It may not be broadcast, published, or made into motion pictures without specific individual authorization in each performance thereof."

Despite this relentless insistence on being given credit for everything, the Hummerts were quiet and reclusive. They lunched together, when in New York, in a Park Avenue restaurant that thoughtfully shielded their table with ferns. Hummert, a tall, thin, rangy man, was likely to order shredded wheat. Anne was always described as well dressed, but whether her clothes were dull and almost Quakerish or simply the height of understated chic has been argued with some heat. One interviewer thought that her "status in the agency was well expressed in her costume"—which he described as a practical red woolen office dress worn with a rope of pearls and pearl earrings.

So independent were the Hummerts, and so powerful, that during the McCarthy era, when everyone else in broadcasting panicked at the very thought of Communism, they went serenely on producing their numerous shows and paying no attention whatever to the famous Blacklist. That list of proscribed actors was slavishly honored by the rest of the industry, who refused any association with the tainted Left; the Hummerts, with their usual efficiency, simply went about their business. Their income was estimated variously at between $300,000 a year and "millions."

Of course Irna Phillips, Elaine Carrington, and the Hummerts did not singlehandedly create the soap opera of this golden age. Many other writers made their contributions, large or small. But theirs was the power, and the glory, and the kingdom of soap.

RADIO SOAPLAND

§

DAVID: But you see, Mad, nobody's ever paid much attention before. Isn't that always the way?

MADELEINE: Sometimes you never miss something that is very dear to you until it's gone. We thought they would go on forever . . . and they practically have.

DAVID: But radio soaps died over ten years ago and most of the scripts are lost forever, living on only in the hearts of their listeners. There are generations growing up now who won't know what we're talking about.

MADELEINE: We must continue—searching, searching, searching.

DAVID: But most of the scripts and the people are dead, or missing.

MADELEINE: Not all, David. Gone but not forgotten. Persevere, mon ami, try that number again. You know, Irna Phillips in Chicago . . .

LIVING

In the golden days of radio, when listening ladies tuned in to their favorite soaps, prepared to eavesdrop on the doings of the families in whom they took so intense an interest, what kind of world were they entering? It clearly resembled the real world, but Soapland had a character of its own. Some aspects of the real world were entirely absent; others were given special significance.

By and large, Soapland is a good place. There is a great deal of violence, to be sure; it keeps bursting through the pleasant surface of life, and there are some people who are mindlessly, irrevocably evil. But generally speaking, if something is wrong it is not immutably wrong. Evil will be defeated. Good people who continue to strive will eventually emerge victorious. They must maintain their faith that the world and the people in it are essentially good, and that happiness is an attainable goal.

The people of Soapland are a varied lot. Some researchers break them down into three classes: the good (mainly women), the bad (mainly rich people, foreigners, and gangsters), and the weak (mostly men). Soap opera writers, on the other hand, have always maintained that their characters are, like all of us, mixed. Part of the interest, they claim, lies in the suspense of following characters who change, evolving into more, or less, strong, good, mature, and happy people.

Truth seems to lie more on the side of the writers; soap characters are more complex than they are usually given credit for being. Even the best of heroines is capable of being wrong: she can misunderstand other people; she can misjudge their motives; she can have an excess of good qualities that leads her into trouble. Men, though far more likely than women to cause trouble on a soap opera (exactly twice as likely, according to one researcher's count), can also be indispensable, full of wisdom, strength, and understanding. Foreigners, meddling mothers-in-law, even gangsters, can surprise us by changing.

Soapland is usually a small town, with a name like Beechwood or Simpsonville, and the residents are strongly attached to it. A young lawyer with a job in New York announces that as soon as possible he intends to return to Springdale and set up his law practice there. Reminded that there are more opportunities of all kinds in the big city, he answers: "I'm not so sure about that. All the things I can think of that I want to do, now and always, lie right here in Springdale."

Clem Betts of *Moonshine and Honeysuckle* admits that he would like to have a look at the world on the other side of the mountains, but would never want to live anywhere but Lonesome Hollow. "I got a heap of contentment," he explains. "I've seen a lot of people from the flat country tother side, and it looks to me they air allus huntin' something. Somehow I feel like hit's these here mountains they air lookin' fer."

When people from the big city do come to small towns, they frequently find peace for the first time in their lives and decide to settle down. This usually happens to wealthy socialites, but people with dubious pasts can also be rehabilitated. Conversely, a yearning for the bright lights and diversions of city life is a sign of poor moral character. The truth is that the big city is all very well for a visit, but a person looking for happiness is more likely to find it in a small place. Small towns are populated, in the main, by good people who understand the real values in life. Gangsters, predatory women, troublemakers of all sorts, come from outside.

There is a story that the redoubtable Anne Hummert once told one of her dialoguers, "I want you to put God on every page." The writer responded, "Who will play the part?" and was promptly fired. Despite what this anecdote might suggest, religion is not important in Soapland. It is respectfully mentioned from time to time. Characters sometimes attend church services. A Bible story may be read to children on a Christmas program. On one show a sermon on brotherhood was presented every year, and the audience could send in for a free copy. Characters may address their soliloquies to God, and sometimes they say a prayer. But religion is not pictured as a driving force in people's lives.

The use of religious terminology is simply a way of setting a seal of approval on certain events and values. Mrs. Dawson, newly returned from a near-fatal trip to New York, after a con man convinced her that she was to be reunited with her long-absent husband and thus tricked her into mortgaging her house and turning the money over to him, wants to express her happiness at being back in Springdale with her family.

"It's good to be here," she says. "It's so good that I—I

wish—Jim, could you say a little prayer before I start my breakfast?'' Jim, a thoroughly admirable man but no churchgoer, complies.

"Well, I can try," he begins. "Dear God, we thank Thee for bringing together this family again—for watching over our beloved Susan Dawson—for keeping her safe when danger threatened her—for bringing her back safely to us. Amen."

On another occasion, when Rosemary and Bill Roberts have just come back from their wedding trip, Rosemary's mother brings God to the table again. "Just a minute, children," she asks. "I want to say grace." She pauses for thought. "God bless these two children who are joined together, and may their life be one of happiness and of service to Thee. May they know great love and the beauty of sacrifice and of compromise. May they live their life to Thy glory. Amen."

In times of trouble, perplexity, or serious illness, God is thought of more frequently. In a soliloquy, a radio mother foresees trouble ahead for her sixteen-year-old son. "I am Ann Davis, Tom's mother," she murmurs. "My cup of worry is brimming over where Tom is concerned. He is so young to be faced with a problem as great as his. I know the intensity of adolescent love and what it can do to a boy, even without the added knowledge that he is responsible for the blindness of the girl he loves. I am so afraid it might cause him to do some rash deed—oh God in heaven, give him strength to keep his head and do Thy will."

The religion of Soapland is a domestic religion that asks no more than simple goodness and, above all, kindness to one's fellowman. These qualities are extremely important and they are frequently demonstrated on soaps, but without any reference to religion as such.

A doctor who, no matter how exhausted, will brave any weather to make a house call is the highest example of this ethical orientation, an embodiment of the Golden Rule, but he need never go to church or even mention God. Women are very often depicted as admirably selfless, too. Molly Goldberg, for one, is an indefatigable do-gooder. She is criticized for excessive altruism by her husband, who asks her,

"Vhat tanks vill you get? Running your feet off far your neighbors, ha?" She replies equably, "To do good tings, dat ain't itself a tanks? Notting no matter vhat you vould do is so sveet like vhen you do someting far somebody."

When it is suggested that the Dawson family take a confused young veteran into their home to rehabilitate him, Rosemary, the working daughter of the household, is reluctant. The house, she feels, is too small; the presence of a stranger would be oppressive, especially for her ebullient younger sister, Patti. But then Dr. Jim, who suggested the idea in the first place, tells Rosemary what her mother's reaction was when the plan was first explained to her: "Jim Cotter, if I can do anything in the world to help any man who's gone through shell fire—who's come back confused and lost and perhaps terrified inside at all that he's done—at all that he's seen—Jim, I'd give my right hand to take care of him. I'd consider it a privilege . . . I'd consider it the greatest privilege I ever had."

Dr. Jim pauses. "That's what your mother said, Rosemary," he continues. "That's why I love her—that's why I'm proud to know her . . . That's why I'm mighty grateful to count myself one of her friends." Rosemary, impressed by this account, asks, "Did Mother really say that?" Dr. Jim assures her that "She certainly did." "Well," concludes Rosemary, having given it time to sink in, "if she said that, I don't see how either Patti or I can object."

Goodness, kindness, and a desire to help other people get out of trouble are among the strongest and most necessary motivations in soap opera. In fact there is a whole class of soap people known, among those who discuss such things, as "helping-hand characters." Characters of this kind have always been an integral part of soap opera plotting; indeed, many soaps are organized around one of them. *Just Plain Bill* had barber Bill Davidson as its pivotal character. Most of the show's problems were really none of his business, but his desire to assist those in trouble—especially his problem-prone daughter Nancy—involved him in episode after episode through the years. Ma Perkins, who has been referred to as "Just Plain Bill in skirts," was another of these helping hands, deeply concerned about the lives of others, but with little dramatic life of her own. Papa David of *Life Can Be Beautiful* spent most of his time in the Slightly Read Bookshop dispensing advice and eliciting information without taking much part in the action; his main function was to remind his ward, Chichi, that, however dismal things might seem at the moment, life could be beautiful. Rosemary Dawson of *Rosemary* started out in the role of indispensable link, sympathetic ear, and helping hand, but soon became involved in the central romance. Years passed, however, and the wild, pulsating love affair settled into a—for soap opera—placid marriage; then Rosemary reemerged as a helper, most of the show's problems revolving around her friends and protégés.

As a device for making a continuing story possible, a central helping-hand character who can connect a number of subplots convincingly is invaluable. Suspense can ebb and flow without ever really being resolved, yet continuity is maintained.

The wisdom of the trade holds that audiences will never fully accept a young helping-hand character. It was tried, long ago, when Ruth Wayne of *Big Sister* was created. Audience interest lagged until Ruth became involved with a married man whose wife was insane. The fact that from that time onward the program became one of the most popular in radio history does not conclusively prove the point; perhaps Ruth could have won acceptance as a helping hand despite her youth, while someone else's involvement with a married man brought the program to the top of the ratings. But insiders in soap opera have always been eager to extract a lesson from events, quick to learn it and pass it along to others. And there is probably some truth to the idea that the audience prefers an older helping hand, since the audience has always preferred most soap characters to be mature.

Young girls have not, as a rule, made successful heroines of soap opera. Experience—which is to say marriage, widowhood, or divorce—seems to be a necessary qualification for audience identification. A heroine can, to be sure, start out as an inexperienced girl, but events will age her quickly. Rosemary is one example of this. Joan Field Davis of *When a Girl Marries* is another. Joan had been on the air only six months when she married Harry Davis in Episode No. 133.

The inhabitants of Soapland who most need the qualities of goodness, kindness, and helpfulness are, not surprisingly, the parents. Parenthood—and this generally means motherhood—is rewarding, but its demands can be immense. It often calls for sacrifice. Soapland mothers traditionally face a choice between motherhood and romance. Mother Dawson, whose husband disappeared sixteen years ago, leaving her to bring up their two daughters, is asked by her teen-ager if she has ever thought of marrying again. "No," she says. "But didn't you ever meet anybody who intrigued you the least little atom?" the child persists. "I was too busy," Mother Dawson explains, "bringing up two babies, to be intrigued by anything but sewing and mending and washing and ironing."

What's more, Mother Dawson has continued to build her life around her children even now that one of them is sixteen and the other twenty-three. She has a suitor, but he will just have to wait till the children marry and leave home. Young Widder Brown, in a somewhat similar situation, could not marry Dr. Anthony Loring unless her children could be won around to the idea. Indeed, her story was billed as "the conflict between a mother's duty and a woman's heart."

Harry Davis's mother lived only for him and his brother Tom, another case of a mother with one child in high school, another grown up, and no discernible outside interests. Harry, a promising young lawyer who has just won his first case, looks at his mother and asks, "Hey, Mother, what are you crying about?" "I'm crying," she replies, "because I'm so proud of you."

Parenthood goes on and on. Vikki Hoyt, though she is married, drops in on her parents almost daily, to resume the role of pampered child. Her mother, in the kitchen busily cooking dinner, tells her not to help. "That's a girl. Now stay there—out of trouble." Vikki, laughing, accuses her of "saying that to me since I was six years old"—and her mother replies, "And do you suppose that I think of you as *more* than that age most times?" Vikki protests, "Even though I am grown up and

married?'' and her mother insists, "Even though you are!''
Whenever Vikki has a problem in her marriage, and she frequently does, she goes straight to her parents to ask their advice.
Occasionally things get so bad that she considers returning
to them permanently.

A similarly close relationship prevailed between Mrs. Dawson and her two daughters when they did eventually marry
and settle down. Family visits were almost a daily occurrence,
and all marital problems were discussed immediately and in
detail. Two generations of the Pepper Young family engaged
in the same round of family visiting and discussion, though
Pepper's wife's family, oddly enough, was never in evidence.

However grown up a child may be, he never outgrows his
need for mothering. Until he marries, he is free to ask for
it. Just before Harry's marriage, he's going through a difficult
time and his mother comforts him with a cup of coffee. "Go
on," says she, "drink your coffee while it's hot. And after
that, you're going to bed and I'm going to tuck you in the
way I used to do when you were a little boy." "Thanks,
Mother," says Harry. "You know what I wish you'd do?"
"What?" "Remember when I was a kid and had nightmares?"
he asks. Indeed she does. "They could hear you yelling a block
away." "Yes," he remembers, "and you'd come in my room
and sit down beside the bed till I went off to sleep again.
Will you do that tonight?" "Yes, Harry," his mother promises,
"I'll do it tonight." The theme music comes up and fades under
the announcer's sympathetic "Well, Harry, we know how you
feel. And you, Mrs. Davis, there to give the help your son
needs."

But the continuing involvement of some mothers in their
children's lives is not so admirable. These are the mothers who
are too involved. Not content to soothe or advise their children,
they try to break up their love affairs, and the point is made
again and again that this is not a good idea. It results only
in unhappiness for the mother because it will lead to estrange-
ment from the child who finally uncovers her machinations
and rejects her.

In the early days of radio soap opera, this total dedication to parenthood at the expense of everything else was held to be necessary. Insiders sagely opined that the soap audience simply wouldn't stand for any other arrangement, a belief derived from the history of a Hummert property, *Betty and Bob.*

First aired in 1932, *Betty and Bob* had all the ingredients of a successful soap. Betty was a stenographer. Bob Drake, her boss, fell in love with her. Disowned by his millionaire father when he married Betty, Bob was clearly unready for marriage or for unwonted, unwanted financial independence. He was attractive to other women. He was jealous. He was immature.

In less than four years the young couple had, the announcer proclaimed, "surmounted everything: divorce, misunderstanding, the interference of other people, and, sometimes the worst of all foes, the passage of time." The Drakes' young son had been the focal point of many episodes, and when, after two years as radio's most popular daytime serial, the program's ratings plunged, suspicion fell on little Bobby.

Audiences, the argument ran, had rejected a plot built on the apparently boundless jealousies of a couple with a child. Boundless jealousy in itself was, to be sure, a most desirable commodity; in earlier days the audience had eagerly followed the story, anticipating the next jealous episode, relishing the most painful squabble. But ratings had plummeted following the birth of Bobby, and radio people concluded that an audience could not be expected to sympathize with a couple so absorbed in their marital problems that they failed to provide a stable and happy home for their innocent child.

Some writers took this lesson to heart and eliminated children from their programs. Childless couples abounded. What children there were in these soap marriages lived subterranean lives, brought forth at Christmas, spoken of occasionally, heard almost never.

Yet children could never be entirely banished from Soapland, since they were frequently demanded by some exigency of plot or in order to establish character. The surest way to tell the good people from the bad ones is by their attitude

Freeman Gosden and Charles Correll, Amos and Andy, in 1928 (TOP) and 1953 (BELOW).

Gertrude Berg in the studio performing the role of Molly
in *The Goldbergs,* which she also wrote.

Virginia Clarke was over thirty-five and looking for love on *The Romance of Helen Trent*. The others are Bill Green (left), Bill Farmer, and Louise Fitch.

Mary Jane Higby was Joan on *When a Girl Marries*, and
Robert Haag was her husband, Harry Davis.

(ABOVE) Vivian Smolen and Karl Swenson
played Sunday and her husband, Lord
Henry Brinthrope, on *Our Gal Sunday*.
Swenson also starred as Lorenzo Jones.

(RIGHT) Joan Tompkins, heroine of *This Is
Nora Drake*, finally married Fred Molina
(played by Bill Quinn) in 1954. In real life
she is married to Karl Swenson.

Virginia Payne (ABOVE) made up as Ma Perkins in 1937; (TOP RIGHT) in a glamour shot taken the same year; (BELOW) and as she appears today.

Anne Elstner, most famous as Stella Dallas, also played
Cracker Gaddis on *Moonshine and Honeysuckle*.

Virginia Kaye was Rosemary on the Elaine Carrington serial. Today she plays Rose Pollack on *The Edge of Night*.

Jan Miner, orphanage supervisor Julie on radio's *Hilltop House*, is now seen on TV commercials as Madge the manicurist.

On *One Man's Family* Mother Barbour, Jack, Claudia, Paul, Hazel, and Father were played by Mary Adams, Page Gilman, Barbra Fuller, Russell Thorson, Bernice Berwin, and J. Anthony Smythe.

Charita Bauer, longtime leading lady of *The Guiding Light* on both radio and television.

toward children. A heroine loves children, preferably her own, but any child will do. As one mountain girl said to another on *Moonshine and Honeysuckle* in 1932, "Funny how us wimin take to babies no matter whose they air." Her friend agrees: "Wimin a-lovin' babies sorter makes the world, I reckon."

A young married heroine, holding a neighbor's baby for the first time, sums it up: "I've never held any baby before. Ummm, it's a wonderful feeling, isn't it? It just seems your arms are full of something you always wanted there."

If a woman truly loves a man, she longs to have his child. Joan Davis, talking things over with her mother-in-law, confides: "I often look at that locket you gave me with Harry's picture in it when he was a baby. I simply adore it. I'd love to have a baby like that someday." The older Mrs. Davis assures her, "I hope you do. You'll never know what fun life can be till you have your own baby in your arms." Joan, pleased, replies, "I love your point of view about everything, Mother Davis. It always seems so *right*."

On another occasion Joan discusses her approaching marriage with her father's secretary, who warns her, "You'd better not be getting any notions that marrying a poor man is any bed of roses." Joan insists that she doesn't think it matters whether a man is rich or poor, "as long as you're in love with him." "That's what you think now," replies the prosaic Miss Gray. "But wait till you have to do your own work and mend your own clothes and take care of your own baby." "Oh, I'd love to take care of a baby," Joan insists. Miss Gray realistically continues: "That's because you never had to. I brought up half a dozen brothers and sisters, and there's nothing romantic about it at all." Joan cannot be shaken. "But your *own* baby, Miss Gray," she says, "a baby that belongs to you . . . a baby that—that looked like his father—wouldn't you adore to bring him up?"

Even a girl who knows her love will never be returned is thinking of babies. A weeping secretary in love with her boss confides in her mother, "I'm not crying because I can't have him. I knew that. But I'm crying because the way I feel about him—the way I love him—is wasted." "Love's never wasted," her mother comforts her. "You said yourself you could help him in lots of ways . . . in more ways than she can ever help him." "Yes," admits the girl, "but that's not what I mean." Pressed for an explanation, she continues: "I mean—I mean, I can never hold a baby of his and mine in my arms. That's what I mean." The mother, taken aback, says, "I didn't know you thought about such things." The girl replies: "Every girl thinks about that when she loves a man."

There are, of course, bad women who neglect children or do not wish to have any. Audrey Roberts, a very bad wife indeed, shows herself clearly for what she is by placing her daughter in something referred to darkly as a "home." When Rosemary hears of it, she knows exactly what kind of woman Audrey will turn out to be.

Good men love babies, too. When Bill Roberts, the amnesic veteran, recovers his memory, his first recollections are of taking care of his little daughter. Clem Betts, left alone with an infant, holds it awkwardly, but clearly it appeals to him. "My Lord," he says to it, "ain't ye little?" The baby coos. Clem laughs softly and continues, "I'll swear I wish ye wuz mine."

Nothing appeals more to a man than a woman who loves children. Joan Davis picks up a little girl who has scraped her knee, and when the child, comforted, has gone home, Joan and her husband discuss the episode.

HARRY: Joan, do you know something?

JOAN: What?

HARRY: I love you more this minute than I ever did before.

JOAN: Why?

HARRY: I don't know. It's got something to do with your running to that kid when she was hurt . . . picking her up out of the dirt and wiping her tears away. I'll never forget it.

JOAN: Oh, anybody'd pick up a child who was hurt.

HARRY: Maybe. But it was the way you looked when you did it. Joan, I hope we'll have a baby someday.

JOAN: So do I—I want a little boy—a little boy to look like you.

HARRY: And I want a girl to look like you—with the same brown eyes.

On the other hand, second-rate men are not so enthusiastic about the idea of having children. Joyce, a secretary whose employer is divorcing his wife to marry her, is looking forward (mistakenly, as events prove) to a lifetime of happiness with the man of her dreams. The audience could certainly tell from this scene that he would prove unworthy of her.

DICK: I know the future holds nothing but fun for both of us. We're going to have a swell time, Joyce.

JOYCE: I know we are. I know it's going to be wonderful . . . I know it's going to be perfect. And Dick, when we have our children—

DICK: Children? No—no children, Joyce. Just you and me. Just the two of us. I don't want to share you with any children.

JOYCE: Oh, but I'd love to have children, Dick. I'd love to have a little boy who looks like you and—

DICK: I'm not in favor of it. I want you to be able to go with me wherever I go at a moment's notice. I want you to be able to toss things into a suitcase and run for a train, whenever I have to run for a train. You can't do that if you're tied down with a family, Joyce.

JOYCE: No, I suppose you can't.

DICK: All my life I've wanted somebody who'd pick up and go places and do things and stay up as late as I like to stay up. That'll be more fun than having children, Joyce. That'll be being lovers for the rest of our lives.

JOYCE: Yes, but—but—

DICK: That's the kind of a girl I want, Joyce, and that's the kind of a girl I know you are. You're my girl and we're going to have a swell life together from now on.

Divorce is, of course, rejected in the ethos of Soapland—but more in principle than in fact. And when people discuss it, their first argument concerns the effect divorce has on children. Sam Field, Joan Davis's father, has been separated from Joan's mother for many years. The separation took place long before the action of the program began, but though Mrs. Field seems content with her estranged state, Mr. Field frequently repines. In this scene he tells Joan's husband that he is a failure as a father.

FIELD: No man who lets his children grow up away from him, no matter for what reason, deserves to share in their lives later on.

HARRY: I disagree with you there, Mr. Field. A man can't always put up with everything. Sometimes he has to get out.

FIELD: No he doesn't. Not where children are concerned. I can say that now, having been one of those who got out. But if I had to do it over again, Harry, I'd make my home hang together, somehow, just so that I could be with those two little girls while they were growing up.

HARRY: They always feel they've got you there, if they need you.

FIELD: It isn't the same thing. A father who lives down the hill in an apartment house may be a kind and understanding person, but it's not the same father who lives under the roof with you. You don't feel the same way about him—you can't. He's walked out on you.

HARRY: You oughtn't to feel that way.

FIELD: But I do, and I'm right about it. I've never told anybody this before in my life, but I'd give everything I have— everything I expect to have—to have stayed in the house on the Ridge with my two little daughters.

HARRY: I don't think you've got a thing to blame yourself for, Mr. Field.

FIELD: That's because you don't know, my boy. You don't know anything about it. You've never lived in a house divided against itself. It not only does something to a man like me but it does something even worse to the children. Oh, you may not see any signs of it in Joan and Sylvia today, but there are scars there, just the same . . . the scars of not having a father when other children have a father—the scars of their mother's bitterness against me. You have a right to do what you like with your own life, but you haven't any right to do it to your children.

HARRY: I see what you mean.

FIELD: Marriage doesn't always work out. It's a clumsy arrangement at best, but it's the best device there is for keeping the family together. You can't toss that overboard and not be punished for it.

Even if there are no children involved, divorce is not to be taken lightly. Marriage is very important. It may demand sacrifice and compromise, but even a mediocre marriage has its compensations. As one soap heroine soliloquizes, "It's such a hopeless thing to see the end of a marriage. I wonder how people can so carelessly sacrifice the only real security that comes in life—a home. If we would only think first, we would never let selfishness or misunderstanding touch our lives. I've seen it happen in my mother's life—I've seen what the years have brought to her, in loneliness. That's why I'm so sure we should all strive to build and keep a peaceful happy home in this world of unrest. It's our security for the future. It's our greatest chance for happiness."

Marriage is not to be tossed lightly aside for a newer, more promising romance, either. Only a permanent commitment can be expected to bring true satisfaction. Dick Phillips, a lightweight man with a long history of unfaithfulness, has decided to divorce his long-suffering wife. "Emily," he puts it to her as prelude to asking for a divorce, "we've been married a good many years, and the bloom is off the rose, isn't it?" Emily, still deeply committed to the marriage, asks, "Is it?" "You know darned well it is," Dick replies. "You know darned well that something goes out of marriage after a while—call it the romance, if you like—I don't know what to call it." Emily counters with "Isn't that when—the partnership begins?" "The partnership?" he asks, bewildered. "Yes," says Emily, "the thing you settle down to enjoy for the rest of your life."

Though the soap consensus is that marriage must be respected, it frequently happens that a husband or wife falls in love with someone else. When the claims of licit and illicit love conflict, there is opportunity for everyone's point of view to be expressed while the question is viewed from every possible angle.

One marital conflict that continued for many months on

Rosemary was the Joyce-Dick-Emily triangle. Originally, the problem is that of the unmarried girl in love with a successful, attractive, older married man. He says he loves her. Can the audience believe that his intentions are honorable? He assures Joyce that Emily no longer has any interest in him and promises he will ask for a divorce. The audience knows, however, that he is putting off this confrontation. Dick lies to Joyce, explaining that he couldn't mention divorce to Emily because she has the flu. The audience, knowing Emily to be in perfect health, can only wonder what Dick's deception means. Does he love Joyce? Does he intend to marry her? Does he instead love Emily?

But then the problem becomes more complex. Dick decides he really wants to marry Joyce and asks Emily for a divorce. The audience discovers that Emily still loves Dick, and the question becomes a moral one: Does Joyce have the right to marry a man who is loved by another woman? This is argued out in episode after episode between Joyce and her friend Rosemary; between Rosemary and her mother; between Rosemary and a suitor of hers, Peter Harvey; and eventually between Joyce and Dick.

Emily comes to Joyce's boardinghouse late at night to tell her she has decided to grant Dick's request for a divorce because she is now convinced that he truly loves Joyce and can be happy only with her. When Joyce sees Dick at work next day, she is still in the throes of remorse and guilt.

DICK: Darling—this isn't the place to tell you—but I want you to know that everything's going to be all right—

JOYCE: Everything? . . . No, Dick, it can't be all right . . .

DICK: What do you mean? It *is* all right . . . I've talked to Emily this morning—and she's consented to everything . . . she's going to make it easy for me . . .

JOYCE: No—no—Dick, you don't understand . . . she loves you . . . she really loves you . . . I didn't know . . . you didn't tell me—

DICK: Joyce, I'm telling you now—she's going to make everything easy for us . . . she's consented to go away—to get a divorce—because she thinks you're right for me, darling . . . Strange, but perhaps the best thing she could have done was to go to see you last night—

JOYCE: No—no, I'll never forget it.

DICK: Joyce, can't you smile for me, darling? . . . Don't you understand? Everything's all right!

MUSIC: *Mood*

ANNOUNCER: Like a woman turned to stone, Joyce stands there as Dick comes forward and takes her hand—as Dick bends over her and kisses her lips . . . Everything all right? How can it be, her heart cries—how can there be happiness in a structure built on a woman's broken heart?

But Joyce pulls herself together and decides she must accept happiness when it is offered. She confides in her friend Rosemary, who is shocked by the ruthlessness of Joyce's decision. Joyce admits that Emily Phillips seems to love her husband deeply, and Rosemary protests.

ROSEMARY: Oh, Joyce, then you can't do it—you can't possibly do it—

JOYCE: That's the way I felt last night, after she left—although she told me that he didn't love her any more—that he only cared about me. Rosemary, just think—she actually came and told me that—

ROSEMARY: It must have broken her heart to tell you that—

JOYCE: She seemed much more concerned with the fact that—that she didn't want him to hate her, that whatever happened, she didn't want him to hate her—

ROSEMARY: Oh, I'm so sorry for her, Joyce—you've got to get out of this thing now. You can't do it. You can't go through with it. Don't you see, you can't build any happiness on her sorrow?

JOYCE: In a strange kind of way I think she'd completely decided to give him up, if she thought I was the right sort of a person—

ROSEMARY: I don't care what you think, you can't do it, Joyce . . . not if she cares for him.

No matter what Joyce says, Rosemary is adamant; she believes it is her duty to save her friend from her own rash impulses.

ROSEMARY: Joyce, you've got to tell him that no matter what he wants, no matter what he offers you, you can't accept it. Believe me, you've got to do this, Joyce.

JOYCE: I can't . . . I can't . . . Rosemary, I was so happy till I saw you . . . I thought you'd understand. I thought you'd agree that as long as they'd talked it over—as long as she'd made up her mind—as long as she told him she was perfectly willing to free him—as long as she'd talked to me—

ROSEMARY: Joyce, where's your sense of decency gone? Where's your sense of honor? Where's your fairness? Joyce, you yourself, with your own lips told me that this woman loves her husband—that she's told you she loves him—

JOYCE: I know—I know—but she says he's through with her—

ROSEMARY: You mean *you're* through with him . . . Joyce, you've *got* to give him up immediately . . . you've got to stop this thing before it goes any further . . . you can't—you can't possibly want a man whose wife still loves him as you say Emily Phillips loves Dick . . .

Rosemary cannot convince Joyce, but she can't stop trying. She returns to the question again and again, placing considerable strain on their friendship. "Someday you'll see," Rosemary warns. "You'll understand that you've broken this woman's heart."

Joyce, her back to the wall, at last produces a coherent argument in her own defense. "That's very dramatic, Rosemary, and very silly to say. It isn't true at all. Maybe he broke her heart long ago—maybe she didn't know how to hold him—maybe she didn't love him enough—maybe lots of things, because I don't believe any man would play around with other women if his wife was everything to him. You know that, Rosemary. You know there wouldn't be room for anyone else —any room in his heart, I mean, for anyone else if his wife were everything to him."

Even this can't sway Rosemary. "All I can say is that you should get out of this man's life immediately, now and forever," she urges. "Goodbye, Rosemary," says Joyce. "I didn't think we'd part this way." "Oh, Joyce," Rosemary implores, "won't you let me talk to you some more? Won't you let me show you what you're doing? Not only to him—not only to her—but to yourself, too. You're destroying *you*. You're destroying the sort of person you are. You've got to be true to yourself, Joycey—you're not the kind of a ruthless girl who could tear a man and his wife apart."

Peter Harvey, Rosemary's longtime suitor, criticizes her gently for interfering in Joyce's life. "Darling," he points out, "it isn't your affair. It's really their affair." Rosemary refuses to admit this. "It's any woman's affair," she insists, "when you see a marriage being broken up."

LOVING

Rosemary had a lot to learn about moral judgment. One of the chief lessons of soap is that love is an irresistible force against which a mere human being is powerless. Love may not precisely justify everything, but it does make certain things inevitable. Passing judgment on the inevitable is the height of irrelevant quibble.

Rosemary, whose heart is still unawakened, is not yet a sufficiently developed person to understand this. As Peter Harvey tells Joyce on another occasion, "You'll find people who have lived, Joyce, deeply and completely, are the most tolerant people. They're the ones who understand. They don't go around judging someone else. They know too well how easy it is to do some of the things you've sworn you'd never do. They know how weak human beings are—how susceptible to temptation, and instead of condemning them, they forgive them."

In this case, Rosemary suddenly acquires understanding of Joyce's plight by falling in love herself, and at first sight too. After her first meeting with Lieutenant Bill Roberts, she stands at the street corner gazing after the bus he's on, murmuring to herself, "What's happened to me?" The announcer ends the program echoing her: "Yes, what's happened to Rosemary Dawson, as she is standing there under the streetlamp, gazing after a departing bus, with a vague feeling as she sees it disappear bearing off Lieutenant Roberts that a part of her has been torn away?"

Rosemary, newly able to take a sympathetic attitude, patches up her quarrel with Joyce. When Joyce reminisces about her first meeting with Dick Phillips, Rosemary understands.

JOYCE: I could hardly talk. I was so struck dumb with love. Oh, but you think that's silly, don't you. You don't believe in love at first sight—

ROSEMARY: I . . . I . . . yes, I do, Joycey . . .

JOYCE: No, you don't, you're just being sweet—but it can happen like that—truly it can—you can open a door and see the man who is going to mean your whole life to you and you know it somehow—you feel it—

ROSEMARY: Yes . . . you feel it.

JOYCE: It's almost as though you had a sixth sense . . . something told you without saying anything that this is your man.

ROSEMARY [*softly*]: Yes . . . yes . . .

When Rosemary admits to her mother that she is in the grip of a new and strange emotion, she also realizes that she can now for the first time understand Joyce's position.

ROSEMARY: It's more as if—as if—I'd found somebody I'd lost a long time ago—as if we'd come together after a long separation—as if we'd known each other in another world and lost each other and—and could never bear to be apart a single minute from now on . . . oh, Mother, what am I talking about?

MOTHER: You're talking about love, Rosemary.

ROSEMARY [*in hushed voice*]: Yes . . . love . . . this is love . . . this is what Joycey's been telling me she feels and I've been so unsympathetic and impatient with her . . . this . . . this is it.

Finally Rosemary is able to apologize to Joyce, rescinding all her moral strictures. "I feel so ashamed of having been so intolerant," she confesses. "I expected you to give up Dick just as if he were only a friend. Why, if anybody told me I had to give up Bill—I'd—I'd rather die. Truly I would—I'd rather die."

Rosemary has found happiness with Bill. Joyce, on the other hand, is not to be so fortunate. Dick Phillips is not the man to make any girl happy, but Joyce does not get the chance to learn this from experience. Emily Phillips, in Reno getting her divorce, is killed in an automobile accident. She has left no note, but everyone knows it must have been suicide. A distraught Dick rushes off to arrange her burial and does not return to Springdale for months. When he does at last reappear, Joyce discovers that he has married someone else.

Soap people do very often love unwisely. The man may, like Dick Phillips, turn out to be a Don Juan. The woman may, like Audrey Roberts, prove to have married for money. Gypsy, of *Moonshine and Honeysuckle,* admits her love for an outlaw who has betrayed her and even tried to kill her. "Clem," she says, "I loved him." "I sorter thought so," he answers. Gypsy continues: "I knowed then he wuzn't worth hit." "I reckon a body a-keerin' don't allus take worth to account," Clem suggests. Gypsy concludes: "Hit's the worth ye want 'em to have, ye keer for. And once a woman loves a man, hit takes more than unworth to tear hit down."

But everyone knows that the most important goal in life is finding the right person and falling in love. Rosemary, in her unawakened days, discusses the future with her mother.

ROSEMARY: What do I want, Mother?

MOTHER: I don't know, dear. What do you think you want?

ROSEMARY: Well, I think I want a little home of my own . . . And I'd like babies. I'd simply adore babies. I hope they'll all look like Patti. I can't think of anything cuter than Patti was when she was a baby. Oh, and let me see . . . Then I guess I want—I want a husband who's somehow different from any of the men I've ever met in my life.

MOTHER: In what way?

ROSEMARY: Oh, I don't know . . . I think I'd want him with all of Peter's dependable qualities—all George Schuyler's good looks and charm—and yet I'd want him to be exciting. Do you know what I mean? Do you think it's terribly wrong to want the man you fall in love with to be exciting to you?

MOTHER: No, dear, I don't think so. I think he's bound to be exciting to you, if you're in love with him.

ROSEMARY: Oh . . . I don't know what I want, Mother . . . I'm so happy to have you home, and it's so nice to sit here and talk to you, sometimes I think I don't want to get married at all.

MOTHER: That's nonsense. Of course you want to get married. Every girl wants to get married.

As Vikki, of *Marriage for Two,* expresses it, "It's all I've ever wanted. A husband . . . like Roger . . . and a family . . . and a little house . . . like the one I was brought up in on Winston Street."

It doesn't take anything special to find love and happiness. It's something that can happen to people at any time, however ordinary their lives may seem. To underline this point, romantic moments are apt to occur in unromantic places on soap operas; humble surroundings are transfigured by the strength of the lovers' emotions. Bill proposes to Rosemary as they look through the refrigerator together for a late snack. Clem tells Cracker he loves her as they are filling a kerosene lantern together. "I'm a-keerin' fer ye, Cracker," he says, and the kerosene drips unregarded.

As Rosemary says, "Lots of people you see together who are married and who look at each other as if they love each other are plain people with plain faces. Now I know that to each other they are the most wonderful faces in the world. They're the most wonderful people in the world. They're not little or plain or pale or tired—they're just wonderful godlike creatures who have been lucky enough to meet each other and to fall in love and to get married."

Love brings bliss and rapture into everyday life. Joyce describes hers to Rosemary just after their reconciliation.

JOYCE: Oh, Rosemary, I'm so happy.

ROSEMARY: Are you, dear? I'm glad.

JOYCE: I never knew what it was to be happy before—not really happy . . . not deeply, warmly happy. Happiness is a funny thing, isn't it, Rosemary?

ROSEMARY [*slowly*]: Yes . . . I guess it is.

JOYCE: Suddenly it comes—just like a ray of sunlight—one minute you've been living in a gray world and then you are living in a world of blazing sunlight. [*Laughs*] I guess I sound goofy, don't I?

ROSEMARY: No, you just sound happy.

JOYCE: Happy! Rosemary, it's when you wake up in the morning with this—this choking feeling of utter joy . . . sometimes it seems as if your body is too small to hold so much happiness crammed into it.

ROSEMARY: Darling, you haven't ever known anything like this before, have you?

JOYCE: Nobody has. Oh, I don't mean that I'm the only person in the world who was ever happy this way—that would be foolish—but I mean nobody unless she's in love with the man who's in love with her can feel it. It's as if—as if—well, as if you belonged to a small society and you can only get in when love has unlocked the door.

Later, when Rosemary and Joyce are comparing notes on their love affairs, Joyce says, "Oh, Rosemary, it's such fun to have you feel that way—it's such fun to have you feel the same way I do . . . to know you can't live without a man, just as I can't live without Dick. Isn't it funny how few people know the way you feel? The way you want one man more than anything else in the world? The way nothing matters but to be near him, being close to him, planning to spend the rest of your life with him?" Rosemary admits, "I've had love all my life, and yet I never came alive until I met Bill."

Together the two girls plan their weddings, and Joyce tells Rosemary, "We've found what everybody else is looking for—we've got it. This is it." Rosemary agrees. "Yes," she says, "this is happiness, isn't it? This is the sort of thing you read about in books but you never expect to feel yourself . . ."

If being in love is happiness, marriage can be ineffable ecstasy. A few days after her wedding Rosemary is asked, "Is it fun being married?" She replies, "Oh, Patti, I can't describe it—I can't even talk about it, it's so wonderful." She can discuss it with her husband, though, and she often does.

BILL: Oh, darling, it's so wonderful to look up and see you there whenever I turn my head.

ROSEMARY: I hope you turn it very often.

BILL: You know I will. Darling, can you believe all this?

ROSEMARY: Of course I can't believe it. It's just like—like

the frosting on your birthday cake—it's just like seeing your Christmas stocking when you open your eyes on Christmas morning. It's just like—

BILL: It's just like heaven on earth, isn't it, darling? That's what it's like.

When people marry, they tend to withdraw from most contact with the outside world, though they may continue to visit their parents regularly. As Vikki says one evening when she and Roger are having dinner with her parents, "I was just thinking how happy I am." Pressed for an explanation by Roger ("Any special reason?") she replies, "Very special, darling. Right now, in this room—I've got the three people I love most in the world—and who love me most." A tear falls. "So why shouldn't I be happy?"

Even parents are sometimes forgotten by the happy couple. Harry suggests to Joan that she "stop in and see your mother and sister" while he's at work.

HARRY: It seems to me you're neglecting your family horribly—

JOAN: I know. Isn't it awful? But somehow it doesn't seem as if I had any family except you.

HARRY: It's funny, but I feel the same way.

JOAN: Oh, I love them all, and I'm glad to see them when they come here, but I'm so glad to have them go, too. It's so much more fun to be alone with *you*. Is that being too selfish?

HARRY: It's speeches like that that make it hard for a man to go to work in the morning.

JOAN: Is it hard for you to go to work, darling? I'm *so* glad.

Rosemary wonders if her family won't feel neglected when she and Bill return to live with them in Springdale, but Bill assures her that they'll understand: "What do they expect of a newly married couple? What do they expect of two people whose one and only thought is to be as close together as they can, for the rest of their lives?"

Rosemary herself had realized earlier how much more important marriage is than anything else. "Marriage is such a wonderful thing," she says. "No matter how nice your family is—and mine is darling—or how much they do for you—I don't think you start to live—until you're married. I don't think life takes on any real meaning, any real purpose, until that time. All the rest of it has been a sort of preparation for marriage."

Once they have him, women want to take care of the man they love. They may do it by cooking, by other forms of housework, by waiting on him hand and foot. Mother Dawson eventually married Dr. Jim Cotter, and their relationship shows what extremes the service ideal of marriage can reach.

MOTHER: I know you're tired. You've been on the go all day . . . first operating up at the hospital and then these late calls. So you come right into the living room and take off your shoes, Jim Cotter, and lie down on the couch there and I'll bring you something on a tray.

DR. JIM: Susie, you just spoil me to death, don't you?

MOTHER: Nonsense—I don't have enough *time* to spoil you. When I start spoiling you, the telephone rings and you're out again in the middle of a downpour. Now give me your coat—there—and get your shoes off, and curl up and take a little snooze while I get something ready. You know you like to take a nap before dinner.

DR. JIM: I sure do. And I like my best girl to wait on me, too.

MOTHER: And she loves to do it. Oh, Jim, we're a very smug, happy couple.

DR. JIM: Oh, we're not so unusual. It's kind of wonderful how *many* happy couples there are around this country.

MOTHER [*laughing*]: Are there? You'd never know it from the papers.

DR. JIM: Yep. Good women and good men who spend their lives together—hundreds and hundreds of 'em.

MOTHER: Well, I certainly feel sorry for any woman who hasn't got a man.

Another part of wifely devotion is to smooth the way for the husband, whatever he may wish to do.

ROSEMARY: I know my husband is going to be famous.

BILL: Your husband is going to be a good reporter—that's all he wants to be.

ROSEMARY: That's not all he's going to be, though. Bill, it

would be so wonderful to—to be married to a genius, as Patti called you.

BILL: Listen, honey—please don't put a tag like that on me.

ROSEMARY: Well, I don't mean that exactly, but I mean just someone who cared about writing, and who had to be protected from disturbances of all sorts. I'd be awfully good at that, Bill —watching over you and keeping the world away from you while you were writing and—and—

BILL: And being near me yourself always, darling. That's all that will ever give me faith enough in myself to work—having you nearby—being able to reach out my hand and touch you.

Sometimes a woman's most important duty is to cheer her husband, help him see things in better perspective. This is Molly Goldberg's constant responsibility. When her husband has business reverses, this is how she responds.

MOLLY: Cool yourself down, Jake darling. Maybe'll be ulleright. My heart tells me.

JAKE: How can it be ulleright? It's a good ting you canceled de new furnitures and ve didn't moved in an expensible flat. Molly, I'm going crazy. I don't know vhat'll be.

MOLLY: I'm surprised from you, Jake. You vhat alvays said never get discouraged, so qvick you lose yourself.

JAKE: But it takes out de starch from a man to get hit in de beginning just vhen everything vas looking so flowering, and I was gonne order far you far New Year's a pair diamond earrings.

MOLLY: Oy, Jake, no matter vhat comes, say like you alvays used to say, "Luck, success, must be mine, can be no odder vay." Just like if you had a mountain to climb, you vould have to put vone foot before de odder and keep on over rocks, over stones, until you got on de top. Be like dat now, and you'll see'll be ulleright.

A wife must try to share her husband's interests and understand what he is doing so she can help his career. Joan Davis talks to her mother about the importance of this, saying, "I'd be ashamed to be a lawyer's wife and not know what he was writing and talking about. That's the trouble with most women,

Mother; they work hard at being interesting and attractive before they've caught their man, but once they marry him, they slump right down and let him go his own way. I'm not going to be like that . . . I'm going to make something of myself and of Harry . . . and I'm going to make his friends like me and make his home a place he can be proud to bring them to." The announcer comments on this in parting: "These are big resolutions of Joan's—and she is sure she can carry them all out, in spite of what her mother says. But will she find, once she has 'caught her man,' that she can live up to them—make a real home for Harry, and be as much help to him as she plans?"

It's important for a wife to treasure every significant moment of happiness, as Joan Davis knows—and makes her husband understand. Harry gives Joan the key to their new house, and she reacts with a few tears.

JOAN: Oh, Harry, my own key.

HARRY: Don't look so tragic, darling.

JOAN: I can't help it, Harry. Do you know it's the first time in my life I've held the key to my own little home in my hand.

HARRY: Joan, you're so darn sweet . . . I wouldn't have thought of that.

JOAN: I want to always remember moments like this forever. You see, Harry, I'm just beginning to realize how important it is to be a wife. What a real job it is.

Of course, a wife must never take her husband for granted. Mrs. Cameron, the pleasant but slightly plebeian woman next door, doesn't understand this clearly, but Joan explains.

MRS. CAMERON: It's nice to be so much in love, isn't it?

JOAN: Heavenly.

MRS. CAMERON: Too bad it can't last.

JOAN: Of course it can if you really want it to.

MRS. CAMERON: I thought so once; oh dear me.

JOAN: But, like every job, it takes work. I think the trouble with most couples is that they start taking each other for granted.

MRS. CAMERON: It's kinda hard not to take somebody for granted that you see around the house all the time.

JOAN: Oh, but you shouldn't. You should think each time you see him, how wonderful it is to have him there, and how dreadful you'd feel if he wasn't there. Then you'd never take him for granted.

MRS. CAMERON: Maybe so, but it's a whole lot more comfortable to let down, and stop feelin' that way.

JOAN: I'm never going to let down.

Women must do what their husbands want. Vikki and Roger Hoyt discuss the problem of husbands who want to move to look for better opportunities.

VIKKI: As long as you put that marriage ring on the third finger of my left hand, Roger . . . you could have taken me anywhere.

ROGER: What a warm, loyal little thing you are.

VIKKI: Loyal? It's a wife's place to go with her husband, isn't it?

ROGER: A lot of wives I know put up an awful squawk when they have to.

VIKKI: Maybe a lot of wives don't love their husbands. I do.

At the end of a long evening of sledding, Rosemary says she's having so much fun she hates to stop. "So do I, darling," says Bill, "but I guess we'd better call it a day." Rosemary shows her womanly subservience, telling him, "All right—you're the boss. You're always the boss, Bill—whatever you say, I'm always going to do."

In return for all this wifely devotion, a great deal is expected from soap husbands. Above all, they must place the same supreme importance on love and marriage that the women do. One way this shows is in their extreme possessiveness.

BILL: I don't want to see anybody—I'm sorry, but I'm selfish about it. I've got to share you with the rest of the world, I suppose—I've got to be unselfish enough to let other people look at you and speak to you and touch your hands . . . But don't you dare look at anybody of the male persuasion for more than half a minute, or I'm not responsible for what I'll do.

ROSEMARY: I don't even know there's anybody of the male persuasion to look at but you.

BILL: No Peter Harvey, mind you. I don't want him hanging around, even though I have won out.

ROSEMARY: You certainly have won out. [*Laughs.*] Poor Peter!

BILL: I didn't know I could feel jealous this way. I didn't know I could feel as if I wanted every bit of you—every bit of your words and your smile and your voice—every bit of your mouth—

ROSEMARY: You have every bit of my mouth—[*Pause. Sound of kiss.*]

BILL: Don't mind me, darling—I just never was in love before.

ROSEMARY: Neither was I.

BILL: Aren't you glad we waited for each other?

ROSEMARY: Oh, how glad I am that we waited for each other.

Good husbands are intensely protective as well. Vikki asks Roger, "When are you going to teach me to drive so I can get my license and call for you every night in the car like a real suburban wife?" Roger demurs, but Vikki persists. "Why won't you teach me?" Roger reluctantly explains: "Because if I do, you'll expect to drive the car while I'm at work . . . I'd worry about you all day—wonder if you were getting into accidents."

A woman need not be a helpless creature, but she appreciates being thought of as one by her husband. Bill's view of Rosemary is unrealistic but welcome.

BILL: You're such a little thing, aren't you?

ROSEMARY: Little—of course I'm not little. What a thing to say. I'm a big girl now.

BILL: I mean, to me, you're tiny, fragile and need looking after.

ROSEMARY: I just love that. Me, tiny and fragile and been out battling for my living ever since I got through school.

BILL: You shouldn't have to do a thing—you should be taken care of—you should sit at home with your hands folded and wait for me to come running up the steps.

ROSEMARY: I never sit with my hands folded—I'd probably be there at the front door waiting to greet you. Oh, Bill, won't it be wonderful when we have front steps of our own? When we have a front door of our own—when we have a house of our own—

A good husband always notices and responds protectively when his wife is worried or unhappy. If Joan is lying awake worrying, Harry senses it and comforts her.

JOAN: I can't get it out of my mind, Harry.

HARRY: Well, we'll fix that. I'm going to turn on the light and you're going to put your dressing gown on and we're going downstairs and I'm going to make you a cup of hot chocolate, and put some logs on the fire, and get you thoroughly sleepy.

JOAN: Harry, it isn't fair of me to wake you up this way. You need your night's sleep, with all the work you've got to do tomorrow.

HARRY: I need to make my little wife happy more than anything in the world. Come on. Put this dressing gown on.

JOAN: Oh, Harry—you're the most wonderful person when I'm scared or worried!

HARRY: I don't know anything about that, but I'm here to look after you, if that's what you mean. Now sit there on the edge of the bed, while I get you your slippers.

A good husband appreciates all his wife does for him and mentions it often. Harry, talking to his mother and a friendly landlady, says of his wife, "She's just as wonderful as I knew she'd be—only more so." The landlady says, "Sounds like you're in love. Ah, me, it does me old heart good to hear you talk like that!" "Well," Harry continues, "if you could see what kind of a housekeeper she's turned out to be and how she does all her own work and watches the budget and doesn't let it run behind, you'd know what kind of a girl I married." His mother adds her opinion: "Yes, I've never seen anybody make more of a success of married life than Joan has. Harry is a mighty lucky boy."

A good husband is vocal in his appreciation of his wife in private, too, often telling her what she means to him.

BILL: Rosemary, I don't believe I could ever have found my way back into the light if it hadn't been for you.

ROSEMARY: It's a lovely night—aren't you glad we're out

together on this lovely night? Oh, Bill, when I think how worried we were about getting married—how afraid you were to let me share your life, I think of it all as a bad dream . . . It's all turned out so beautiful—so radiant—so different from what you were afraid of.

BILL: It's you who've made it that way, honey . . . just you . . . just your faith in me—just your love for me. I tell you, someday I'll write the story of what you've done for just one guy—

ROSEMARY: For the one guy in the world I love better than anything else—

BILL: Yes, my darling. And it'll be a story all about you. I'll try to put every bit of you into it . . . your faith, and your love, and your strength, and the way you laugh . . . Most of all I'll try to put into it the way you laugh—

Marriage, for men and women alike, is the center of life. Since it is so important and so intensely interesting, it is only natural that there should be a huge audience always watching with curiosity to see how it is working out, judging its intensity, assessing the joys and sorrows it brings to the principals. Everyone envies two people in love.

To one engaged couple having their pictures taken together the old photographer says, "It is good to see two young people who are so happy. I was happy once—a long time ago." The girl assures him, "I'm glad you were happy, too," and the old man goes on: "Yes, but my wife, she's dead. Life is no good when your partner is dead."

A father, talking to his newlywed daughter, cautions her: "I know he loves you more than anything else in the world, honey . . . That's the most priceless thing any two people can have, Vikki—this mutual love. You've got it. Don't lose it. Hold on to it—build your life around it."

The outside world is eager to encourage and admire romance. Rosemary and Bill, married, return to a restaurant, the Wishing Well, where a good deal of their courtship took place.

WAITRESS: Is there anything else you two want?

BILL: Not a thing. We have everything in the world.

WAITRESS [*laughing*]: I can tell that. My, but it does me good to have you come in here. I just sort of feel as if your romance started in here.

ROSEMARY: So do we.

WAITRESS: I remember the first time you came in. I knew then you two were in love.

ROSEMARY: Did you? We didn't even know it ourselves.

BILL: I knew I hadn't any right to be in love with you, but love is a funny thing. It has nothing to do with "rights." It just takes you by the heart without asking your permission.

ROSEMARY: Takes you by the heart—that's nice . . . My husband's a writer, you know.

WAITRESS: He is? Well, I might have guessed it . . . You have that sort of a—well—dreamy look, sometimes, Mr. Roberts.

BILL: I only have that dreamy look when I'm looking at my wife—when I'm trying to figure out why in thunder she married me when she had the whole world to pick from.

ROSEMARY: Why I married you? Why, Bill, you didn't have a chance of getting away from me once I found you again.

WAITRESS: Did you lose him, Miss?

ROSEMARY [*laughing*]: I think I lost him in another existence. I think we were together a thousand years ago, and then we were parted. And suddenly I found him in this existence and I knew then I'd never let him go again.

When Joan's father comes to visit, Joan and Harry Davis demonstrate their happiness before an ideally receptive audience.

JOAN: Harry's dying to try out his new song on you. It's dedicated to me. It's called "I Adore You."

HARRY: With an inspiration like Joan, how can anybody help writing anything?

JOAN: Sing the words, too, darling. They're wonderful.

When the song is over and Joan's father is asked how he liked it, he takes the opportunity to sum up his feelings about Joan and Harry's marriage. "I like everything about it and about this place and about you two young people. Do you know that in the compass of this little room you've got the whole world to swing at your wrist? You've got everything. You don't know how I envy you. You don't know how the world envies you. You don't know how beautiful it is to sit by and watch you two, utterly and completely happy."

Joan protests, "It makes us sound awfully selfish," and her father continues earnestly: "Then be selfish, if by being selfish you can guard this happiness and treasure it. It's something that'll never come back to you again, once you lose it. Oh, children, be so careful. Don't ever let yourselves grow apart."

WORKING

Since Soapland is meant to reflect the real world, certain basic correspondences between the two must be maintained. Just as people in the real world work, so the people of Soapland must support themselves as they go about their romances, adventures, and assorted escapades. Most of the men and a number of the women are employed.

But work hardly affects the development of the story line; it is not of central importance to anyone but the occasional neurotic in Soapland. The fact of employment is simply one more device to establish soap characters as real people and to help the audience identify with them.

Soapland's men are usually lawyers or doctors or journalists, scientists, ministers, financiers, and industrialists, not to mention a good many gangsters who do very well for themselves in the crime world. There are always more officers than privates in the work force. Very occasionally, someone from a humbler sphere of life is introduced, but he is unlikely to be an important character.

Some of the men have occupations that are never clearly defined. They run factories that make unidentified products, sell or promote items and services that are never mentioned. Promotions come through or fail to; somebody loses a job or is transferred to Chicago. Sam Young, father of Pepper, occasionally takes a trip in connection with his nameless career, and in one episode he announces upon his return that "the survey proved just what I thought it would. It's simply that our product isn't widely enough known. It needs an introduction and if it gets it, I think it will sweep the country. Everywhere I went they were interested and wanted to hear more about it and see samples." But the audience is never told what "our product" is. (Incidentally, Mr. Young changed careers in later life, becoming president of the Elmwood bank.)

Most of the men are not, on the evidence, enthusiastic about the work they do. Little of their lives seems to be devoted to it. Just Plain Bill shaves mighty few customers because he is too busy running around solving their problems. Men are almost never shown actually working. When we see them in action, they are devoting their thought and emotion to non-professional subjects. Even at office or factory, they are infinitely distractible; when they are not being interrupted by a crisis, they are likely to be revolving questions of a personal nature in their minds.

A man's job seems to bring him little satisfaction; on the contrary, it is apt to introduce complications into his life. A job can throw him into constant contact with women other than his wife. Or jealousy may be aroused by outstanding success at the job, and the jealous person may be expected to make trouble in a variety of ways. Jobs and promotions are won or lost as a result of personal relationships; usually a man fails not because of professional incompetence but because somebody was against him, working to wreck his career.

Once in a while, too, a man's involvement with his work can conflict with his central emotional commitments. Harry Davis becomes so immersed in a legal problem at the office one evening that he decides to work late and break a date with Joan. Her hostile mother fails to give her a message to that effect, and Joan is deeply upset by what she interprets as Harry's neglect. When the misunderstanding is straightened out, Joan with great effort restrains herself from expressing jealousy of Harry's work, and her father commends her for it. "Baby," he tells her, "you're right to give a man his head when he wants to dig into a piece of work. That's a side of a man that's entirely apart from you. You can never compete with it any more than it can compete with you. To be a thoroughly well-rounded fellow, to be the kind of man you can look up to and be proud of, he's got to love his work almost as much as he loves you. He's got to want to stay with it day in and day out." (It should be pointed out here that Mr. Field, himself a lawyer, seems to maintain office hours for the sole purpose of advising Joan about her romantic problems.)

The announcer sums it up thus: "So, for the first time, Joan is up against the fact that Harry's work will play an important part in their life together . . . Will Joan be able to really adjust herself to this new angle of life, or will it bring eventual unhappiness into the lives of these two people who today are so much in love?"

Actually, the love of work is a feeble and flickering flame indeed, compared with the incandescence of Harry's love for Joan. When they reconcile after their misunderstanding, it is clear which will win out.

HARRY: Oh, my sweet, I honestly thought my life had come to an end when I left you tonight.

JOAN: Oh, please, let's not talk about it.

HARRY: Darling. I didn't see any way to go on.

JOAN: Oh, Harry . . . [*Pause.*]

HARRY: The only thing in the world I felt was the fact that I had let you down . . . My Joan . . . the one person on earth I love.

JOAN: It makes me feel so guilty when you say that. I should have been thanking my stars for having a boy like you, a boy who knows how to work.

HARRY: Anything I ever amount to, Joan, will be because of you.

Soapland women work too. A widow or a woman abandoned by her husband has, after all, no choice: she usually has several children to support. She may run a boardinghouse or teach school until the children are old enough to take over. Then she can retreat, or advance, into the traditional mother-domestic role.

Young women work before marriage, partly out of necessity,

partly to meet men, and partly because they enjoy it. Even a wife-mother can emerge from her cozy kitchen and take a job if money is urgently needed. Mrs. Dawson works part time in a jewelry store in order to help pay off the mortgage on the Dawson house. Her high school daughter works after school.

When a woman has a husband to support her, however, her job may become a problem. The woman is supposed to go on to a higher destiny, cooking, washing, and generally drudging for her man. Rosemary, a working girl, argues the point with her new husband.

ROSEMARY: I love my job—

BILL: Never mind your job—you're going to give that up.

ROSEMARY: I am not. The idea—of course I'm not going to give up my job.

BILL: Of course you are.

ROSEMARY: But Bill, I have no intention of giving it up—it's a good job. I don't know what Mr. Selden would do without me.

BILL: He'll get somebody else, of course. What do you suppose people do about a girl when one leaves and gets married?

ROSEMARY: But, Bill—

BILL: I don't want you to work, darling—I don't want you to have to do a thing—just be waited on hand and foot.

He explains that he wants to take care of her and support her, now that they are married. Her responsibility is to give him the necessary faith in himself and his ability to earn a living. "You don't have to worry about me, darling," he assures her. "Now that we're married—now that I have you, back of me, believing in me—" Rosemary answers, "Oh, I do believe in you," and Bill assures her, "I'm sure I could do anything. I'm sure I could go out and lick the world with one hand tied behind me."

Eventually, they compromise; since there is no housework for Rosemary to do as long as they live with her mother, they will both work until they can have their own home. And indeed when they do, many years later, achieve this goal, Rosemary becomes a full-time homemaker, even though the couple have no children.

A girl without a husband may find satisfaction in work, even though a job may not be strictly necessary from a financial standpoint. Eve Stanley, separated from her husband, Phil, needs something to occupy her mind as well as demonstrate her independence. Her solution is to ask her father for a job in the family department store.

EVE: I want a job in the store.

FATHER: You don't have to work, Eve.

EVE: I want to, Father. I want to learn responsibility and the feeling of earning your own money.

FATHER: Yes, that's a good idea.

EVE: I've just suddenly realized the importance of this store to us, as a family, and with that realization has come a desire to work in it. I love a home and all that goes in it. Don't you think, Father, if I begin at the bottom to learn—I can be of help to you? Maybe in the home furnishings—or—

FATHER: Eve—my daughter.

EVE: Please let me work for you?

FATHER: Eve, this is a very happy moment in my life. I want you to.

Later, Eve tells her friend Joan about her new career. "Think, Joan—I'm going to work for a while in every department. That's how I'll learn what it's all about, and then maybe I can buy for one of them and someday perhaps I'll be a manager. Oh, Joan, don't you see—there's no limit to where I can go."

Joan reveals her reaction to all this in a soliloquy later: "It is amazing. Eve hasn't talked of Phil all afternoon. It's like a new world has opened up to her—this thought of a job—and deep in my heart I know it will bring her happiness. It never would me. My life is built around love; all I ask is to have Harry near me, and someday the clutching of little fingers onto mine. I pray only for the security of my own home."

Of course if Eve's marriage had not broken up, she would have remained a contented housewife; the audience of *When a Girl Marries* well knew that Eve was, given the right conditions, a dedicated homemaker.

Working girls who are in love are hardly conscious of the fact that they are working, since romance occupies their minds to the exclusion of everything else. This is equally true of the requited and the unrequited varieties of love and the interesting and dull varieties of employment.

BETTY: When you're in love with somebody, no matter how hard you try, you can't think of anything else.

MOTHER: Of course you can. You've got your work to do. You can think about that.

BETTY: That doesn't matter. Nothing matters. You can have work and play and friends and family filling up your time, but the thought of him will run through the pattern of your life like a scarlet thread. It will be with you every hour you're awake . . . every hour—

Joyce, a working girl, finds her life completely dominated by love; she is hardly aware of anything else, as she explains to her friend Rosemary, who has come to meet her at her office. "Come on, let's get outdoors," she says. "Not that I don't love every stick and stone of this bank where I met him and fell in love with him and he fell in love with me—darling bank! I never go home nights without patting its walls. If I could put my arms around the bank, I'd hug it. There." Rosemary asks her if she ever gets any work done, and Joyce laughingly answers, "Work? You mean in the office? Oh, yes. Some. There's a sort of subconscious that gets work done—that takes over when your mind stops functioning . . . that answers telephones and takes dictation and transcribes notes—while the real you is simply soaring up there in the clouds."

The highest destiny, obviously, is to devote one's life to love. And this applies as much to men as to women. A man's deepest happiness is found, the soaps constantly remind the audience, in his relationship with his wife and, eventually, his children. As Mrs. Davis says, "From the time her son is a little baby in her arms, a mother begins to think about the baby girl who's going to make or break his life . . . All I could hope was that you'd have sense enough to pick out the right kind of a girl, and that's exactly what you've done."

The central importance of marriage for men is explained by Molly Goldberg. Her husband, Jake, is vehement in agreement that unmarried life is no life at all.

TOBIAS: What do I want to get married for, Mrs. Goldberg? I like my freedom. I like to be able to go and come as I please.

MOLLY: But you should get married. It's lonesome, ain't it?

TOBIAS: Oh, I've lots of friends.

MOLLY: Oy, but to have no vone to love and no vone who loves you! Look, vhat vould ve be, Jake, if I didn't had you and you didn't had me? No Rosie, no Sammy, no medals, no *bar mitzvahs*?

JAKE: You got right, Molly. I vouldn't be notting but a shadow; I vouldn't be a real man. I can't even picture to mineself dat I should be a single man. I'm telling you, Tobias, you tink you're free? You only imagine it.

MOLLY: Vhy shouldn't you have a home, full of hearts and faces dat's yours and you is deirs? Oy, a man vidout a child—dat's a sadness!

The importance of women in man's life is demonstrated over and over. They are needed, on the most basic level, to tend a man in marriage as his mother did in childhood. As Harry admiringly tells his mother, "If you could just see Joan getting up at the crack of dawn this morning to get my breakfast as if she'd been doing that all her life. She won't let me do a thing."

But far beyond that, a woman is necessary to a man because only through her can he achieve self-respect. Only a woman's love can give a man the inner security he needs in order to function effectively.

BILL: You've freed me, darling—you've freed me from fear—

ROSEMARY: Oh, Bill—oh, Bill, my love, if I really thought that—if I really thought I could do that for you.

BILL: You have done it, darling—I'm not afraid of anything now—I'm not afraid even of what the past will bring to me someday—because I feel so safe and happy and glad to be here with you. Rosemary, I did need you more than you know—I couldn't let you know how much I needed you—I didn't dare. I was afraid to tell you for fear then you'd take pity on me.

ROSEMARY: Oh, darling, darling, how I love to hear you say this.

BILL: I needed you with all of my heart and soul. I needed your love, darling, and your strength and your faith in me.

Harry Davis, thinking his wife dead, despairs. "It's just the awful realization of my loss," he says, "of the years of the future I have to live without her help—without her guidance."

Soapland women are strong and able in many areas. They may put careers aside when they marry in order to devote themselves fully to wifehood, but this should not for one moment be taken to imply that they could not do all kinds of other things if they happened to want to. Women who have no husbands can have successful careers. Helen Trent, when she was not fending off would-be ravishers, was a dress designer. Ellen Brown supported herself and her children by running a tearoom. Bess Johnson, heroine of *Hilltop House,* was the matron of an orphanage. Portia faced life as a successful lawyer. Mary Marlin was married, but since her husband, Joe Marlin, was amnesically wandering through Asia, known only as the mysterious Mr. X, she was a single woman for all practical purposes. When she replaced Joe as a senator, she achieved more political clout than he ever could have, since her advice was frequently sought by an admirer of hers, the President of the United States. And Mary Noble, originally a stenographer, when an emergency made it necessary, took over a starring role and acted her husband (Larry Noble, Broadway star and idol of a million other women) into a corner.

Women are impressive in less exalted spheres as well. Often when things look darkest, inspiration comes from them. When Harry Davis has reached a dead end in his quest for information about the background of a local teen-ager, only his mother has the wit to think of asking a woman they know who lives right across the street from the subject. Harry, deeply impressed by this intuitive grasp of the situation, recognizes that he himself would never have thought of it.

Wives and mothers frequently have business acumen as well as insight into personal and psychological problems, and fortunately they do not hesitate to set their sons, husbands, and lovers straight, though usually in a tactful way, of course. Their judgments are likely to be correct, and when trouble comes, they, being more resourceful and flexible than men, are often able to come up with a solution.

Men are rarely shown helping women out of their difficulties. It is the other way around. The truth is, men may seem strong, but they all have their weakness. Not only do they lack confidence in themselves, but they are often, for one reason or another, in need of practical help from women. In the case of Rosemary and Bill, Bill spends much of his time confined in a hospital. This forces Rosemary to undertake a variety of dangerous missions on his behalf. For example, she must trace his lost child while he, back at the hospital, waits helplessly for a phone call from her. She risks her life among sinister underworld characters who abduct her and threaten to kill her while Bill, in a perfect reversal of the male-female stereotype, longingly awaits her return.

A remarkable number of accidents befall men in Soapland. This fact may be obscured by the remarkable number of accidents that befall women, but the dependency and helplessness of men are not traits commonly dealt with and emphasized outside of soap opera. Chichi of *Life Can Be Beautiful* loved a man already wheelchair-bound when she met him, and countless other Soapland heroines married men who subsequently became crippled, blind, amnesic, or otherwise incapacitated. In soaps there are large numbers of dependent men, hovered over, protected, saved from death—and loved—by strong, resolute, self-reliant women.

Academic critics enjoy the notion that such infirmities are symbols of male impotence. These men who are so frequently subject to paralysis, they suggest, convey to the listening women the idea that they have no sex life with the heroines. It seems more reasonable, however, to suspect that the idea conveyed is one of encouragement to womanly strength. Being the helpmeet of an incapacitated man justifies a heroine in many activities that would otherwise be forbidden. She can undertake all kinds of adventure for his sake without sacrificing a whit of her true femininity. As long as she is not competing with a man but acting as his surrogate, she can use all her aggressiveness.

Another satisfactory reverie induced by the thought of a male immobilized in a wheelchair may well be that of his assured fidelity to the heroine. Now securely owned by his rightful wife, he is no longer likely to fall victim to the wiles of other women. It is not marital but extramarital sex that is decisively ruled out. And extramarital sex is an ever-present threat. There are many unscrupulous women in Soapland, and men cannot resist them.

These women are brilliant, beautiful, and, above all, determined. Pamela Tower, a successful model, was Roger Hoyt's lover for many years. During a break in their relationship he meets and marries a young and innocent girl. Pamela, realizing that Roger is the only man for her, plots ruthlessly to get him back. First she inveigles him into partnership with her in an advertising agency; once she has arranged things so that they are in daily contact, she has countless opportunities for seduction. The old attraction between them soon reasserts itself.

The unscrupulous other woman is usually to be found working with her victim; she first attracts him with her brain. Claire O'Brien works with Harry Davis as a legal secretary; it is not long before she succeeds in luring him out to a mountain cabin, where they are snowed in and must spend the night together. Later, unscrupulousness is briefly rewarded; Harry, believing his wife dead, marries Claire.

The stay-at-home listener was well aware of the insecurity of her own position. The thought that her husband, in the outside world, was constantly subject to temptation must have been extremely worrisome. As she listened to her favorite soap, she must have derived considerable satisfaction from the thought of a man so crippled and helpless that he was perfectly safe from all outside interference.

The fact that no man can resist temptation is a key to soap opera's double view of men. On the one hand, they are presented as the most desirable of life's rewards. They are admirable, marvelous human beings, full of tenderness, romance, poetic impulse, and, above all, passionate fidelity;

they are able to cherish, understand, enjoy, desire, and respond to a woman just as she would wish, and even beyond. On the other hand, they are incomprehensible, weak, and untrustworthy. They make women suffer. Their feelings change without warning or even explanation. They must be watched incessantly, because it is their nature to roam. Soapland is full of women bereft; there are few such men. A man, abandoned for any reason by a woman, has no trouble finding a new object for his affections. Women's feelings, apparently, are deeper and more durable.

Inescapably, then, there is always a hidden, darker side to love. The emotion that brings such apocalyptic happiness to Soapland's women is also the source of their greatest pain, fear, and suffering.

Falling in love in the first place is a frightening business. It is a venture into unknown and uncharted territory. Rosemary, who has never been in love, is afraid of the changes it can bring. After a warning about what may be in store for her once she finds out what love is, she talks over the ominous possibilities with her fickle little sister, Patti.

ROSEMARY: He said—girls like me—once they—they get themselves tangled up—he meant—in love with somebody—they'd love hard enough to move heaven and earth—because, he said, they never stop to count the cost.

PATTI: Well, don't you think that's nice?

ROSEMARY: I don't know—it sounds like such an extravagant way of loving—I mean, as if you loved much too much—as if you loved much too hard—

PATTI: But I think you would, Rosemary, if you ever really fell for somebody . . . I don't see how you can stay out of love as long as you have, but—but I bet when you *do* fall in love, it's going to be something.

ROSEMARY: Yes—that's what I'm afraid of . . . it's going to be something—

PATTI: Maybe it's better, after all, to be the way I am—sort of on again, off again, if you know what I mean?

ROSEMARY: I'm sure it's better to be the way you are, darling. I'm sure that's a much happier way to be.

Once in love, a girl must always be ready for pain. Joyce

asks her friend, "Oh, Rosemary, why does someone who loves you have so much power to hurt you?" Rosemary, in love by now, knows the answer: "Because he has complete power over you. You hand the person you love the power to make you happy or to make you sad—it's all in his hands." And Joyce, who knows what hurt love can bring, warns: "Never let him go away from you—you never know where they'll go or what will become of your love—once they go away from you."

As Rosemary says to her mother, "Oh, Mother, it's wonderful to love someone so much; but it's a little frightening, isn't it?" Her mother answers, "Of course it's frightening, dear. It's always frightening to—to find that you no longer belong to yourself." Rosemary feels the truth of this and agrees that when you're in love "all of you belongs to someone else. It's so much more important what happens to Bill than what happens to me—so much more important that he's safe and well and happy than that I am."

Because the entire person is invested in the love affair, the specter of total loss can never be too far distant from the happy couple. Rosemary says, "Oh, Bill, I just love to hold hands with you . . . And when you let go of my hand, I just feel —lost." He answers, "I know what you mean—as if part of you were torn away." Only when the two of them are together can their lives have any meaning. "It's funny," Bill muses, "how you suddenly find somebody with whom you want to be every minute, day and night . . . who—who fills up every part of your life . . ."

As Rosemary puts it to Bill on another occasion, "Darling, don't you know yet that when two people love each other the way we do—they both lean on each other—they both need each other—and they cannot live without each other!" If the man cannot be trusted—and he never completely can be—such utter abandonment must be terrifying.

Even the most satisfactory marriage is never safe from jealousy. How, after all, can a woman be sure that a man will not suddenly, incomprehensibly, change his feelings? The anxiety that underlies the desire to create the perfect marriage with its final security gets much of its energy from the fear of loss. Thus all wives are subject to attacks of painful doubt.

Rosemary, apparently perfectly happy in her marriage to Bill, begins to worry the minute she learns that he has a female research assistant. Before she ever sets eyes on the girl, she is jealous of whatever relationship her husband may establish with another woman.

Once the danger is past, she discusses her misgivings with a family friend, who expresses surprise. "You were afraid of anybody taking Bill away from you? You must be crazy, Rosemary! He's mad about you." Rosemary remains skeptical. "I think," she maintains, "every woman is afraid of someone being more attractive to her man—of someone moving in and seeming new and exciting to him." The friend rejects this idea. "But Bill? For Pete's sake, he's devoted to you! He wouldn't *look* at another woman." Rosemary has the last word: "I don't know . . . I couldn't be sure . . ."

Because no woman can ever be sure of her husband, women must take on the conscious responsibility for working to hold their marriages together. Joan Davis explains this to her sister, Sylvia, who has reason to think her husband is unfaithful.

JOAN: When a married man comes to the point that another woman can take him away from his wife . . . the trouble's been going on for a long, long time . . .

SYLVIA: That's ridiculous!

JOAN: No it isn't. The wife has either neglected him or lost interest.

SYLVIA: And what about the husband's interest?

JOAN: Darling, we women are only kidding ourselves if we think for one minute anybody but us keeps the home together . . . it's man's instinct to wander. And it's our job to hold on.

Eve Stanley, abandoned by her husband, nonetheless accepts all the blame for their breakup. An attractive widower invites her, along with Joan and Harry, to dinner at his house.

EVE: You'll wish you hadn't invited me. I'm really not fit

to go anywhere. You see, Mr. Anderson, I happened to be in love with my husband. I still am. Nobody else will ever make any difference to me.

ANDERSON: I like you for saying that. I can't for the life of me understand any man who had your affection letting you go.

EVE: No—[*voice breaks*] I'd rather not talk about it, if you don't mind.

JOAN: Then I'll talk about it. Eve's been the biggest peach in the world through this whole business. It wasn't *her* fault that they broke up. She isn't to blame for anything.

ANDERSON: I'm sure of that.

EVE: Of course it's your fault when your marriage fails. You can't get out of it just because your friends want to bolster you up. I didn't know how to hold Phil and that's why he left me. But that doesn't make any difference in the way I feel about him. I'll always love him—I'll never love anybody else.

The woman will work to save the marriage, but it is recognized that marital problems are usually of the man's making. Joan's sister and her devoted servant discuss the rift in Joan's marriage that ensued from a series of offenses by Harry against Joan, including the famous night spent snowbound with the unscrupulous Claire O'Brien.

LILLY: I'd count on Miss Davis honey gettin' Mr. Davis back in hand any day.

SYLVIA: If they were just let alone.

LILLY: Honey, they is really two people in love.

SYLVIA: I certainly know Joan is.

LILLY: So's Mr. Davis.

SYLVIA: I just don't understand him taking Joan for granted the way he does.

LILLY: Still, Miss Sylvia—

SYLVIA: He's always done it, Lilly. Ever since they were married Joan always had to go through her troubles alone. Harry was always off someplace when she needed him.

LILLY: He didn't do it deliberately.

SYLVIA: I know that—but he's been so thoughtless.

LILLY: Did you ever know a man who wasn't?

The soaps, then, offered the homebound listener a dramatization of the conflict she might be expected to have in her own mind about the nature of men, marriage, and the woman's role. And they suggested that they might have useful answers to the questions a woman was asking herself. As one introduction seductively put it, "To hold a man's love, what should a young wife be? Business partner? Dancing companion? Playmate? Should she place her home and her children above all else? How can she make her life secure from her rivals? These are some of the questions the modern woman faces . . . some of the questions that must be answered . . . when a girl marries."

TWILIGHT OF THE SOAPS

§

[DAVID *is discovered standing alone before a broomstick which has been propped up in a wastebasket. He mumbles into it as if it were a microphone. He holds the last page of a script he has been reading; then, finishing it, he lets it drop, professionally, to the floor.* MADELEINE *knocks, then enters.*]

MADELEINE: Oh, hi. I hope you don't mind my dropping in like this. I happened to be passing by on my way over to—

DAVID: Wait a minute! What's this I-just-happened-to-be-passing-by business?

MADELEINE: I have to give some excuse for being here, just like they always do on the soaps.

DAVID: Once a writer, always a writer.

MADELEINE: How's everything looking, rosy?

DAVID: You can call me David.

MADELEINE: I mean the book. The book! How's it going?

DAVID: Fabulous. Just wonderfully. Isn't that wonderful?

MADELEINE: Yes, but I must maintain my cool. I mustn't be too happy. I am the leading lady, you know.

DAVID: Yes, I know. But be joyous. We are halfway there on our journey, *Write to Happiness.* I've been having a good cry over all these old radio scripts. How lucky we were to find them! Aren't you happy, too, Mad?

MADELEINE: Yes, but if I am joyous and you are joyous that can mean only one thing.

DAVID: That we both are joyous?

MADELEINE: No. That disaster is surely around the corner.

DAVID: You've been listening to too many soap operas.

MADELEINE: You think so? That golden age of radio soaps that you're so joyous about didn't go on forever, you know.

DAVID [*Suddenly sober. A long pause. He takes MADELEINE gently by the hands.*]: Oh, no, Mad, I'm sorry. I didn't know. Is there anything I can do?

MADELEINE: Read the next chapter.

The radio soap era, golden as it was, was not to last forever. The bubble did not exactly burst, but the level of the suds was slowly and surely going down. On the surface, all was calm. The number of soaps hovered around thirty. Advertisers loved them. In fact, they were a great advertising bargain, offering as they did a cost per thousand impressions as low as forty-nine cents. And those impressions were strong. The soap audience was loyal. Ratings were high. The only network competition they had was Arthur Godfrey. And they were still selling soap.

But television by now was thriving, and indirectly it posed a threat to the lives of Ma Perkins, Helen Trent, Sunday, and the rest. Fighting for their own lives against the competition of TV, local radio affiliates were turning away from network programing. If they were to compete successfully with the new medium, they had to sell their time at the highest possible rate; they made more by selling locally than they could by carrying the offerings of their network. The affiliates wanted fewer network shows, to liberate more time for local sale.

Accordingly, the networks cut back. In 1959 CBS lowered network programing from sixty-three to thirty hours a week. Four of its ten serials (*Backstage Wife, Our Gal Sunday, Road of Life,* and *This Is Nora Drake*) were discontinued. They were promptly and profitably replaced by local music programs.

Even this drastic pruning, however, was not enough. Local stations continued to clamor for their freedom. By 1960 the radio soaps had reached the end of their dramatic, suspenseful story line.

There was no way, really, to end a soap, plotted as they

all were for infinity. So many little clues and doubts and hopes about such a number of characters and situations had been implanted in the audience's mind that Arachne herself could not have tied up all the threads neatly. But heroic efforts were made not to disappoint the soap listener by abandoning her in the midst of a never-to-be-finished story.

During its last few months *Rosemary* relied on a number of overlapping and intertwining problems, in thoroughly typical soap fashion. When the decision was made to bring its ten-year history to a close, it was impossible to resolve all the established conflicts. The story had to be simplified into a central question, one that could be answered to the listener's satisfaction. A summary of *Rosemary's* final months suggests the difficulties involved.

The heroine, Rosemary, and her husband, Bill Roberts, editor of the Springdale *Banner*, are living happily in the little town of Springdale, which is apparently equidistant from New York and Chicago. The only shadow in Rosemary's life is that not very long ago she lost an ardently longed-for baby. This vacancy in her heart has been partially filled, however, by the Robertses' virtual adoption of two young people, Anna and Lonny Cisare.

Bill, through his editorials in the crusading *Banner*, has cleaned up Springdale, previously victimized by a political boss who ran the place with the aid of a gang of hoodlums, and started a Boys' Club to help the young fellows who had been hanging around the pool hall make something of themselves with the cooperation of local businessmen.

Anna, despite a long period of doubt that she was worthy of him, marries the assistant editor of the *Banner* and begins a life of marital bliss, raised to the plane of ecstasy by almost instantaneous pregnancy. Lonny stays on with Bill and Rosemary, and is elected treasurer—apparently its highest office—of the Boys' Club.

Lonny gets involved with a worthless but irresistibly attractive girl somewhat older than he. Bill and Rosemary discuss the problem with him and believe they have helped him extricate himself from this unwholesome relationship. Actually

Lonny continues to see the worthless Monica, playing hooky from school in order to do so. By the time Bill and Rosemary find out that this boy in whom they have placed their trust, and whom they were hoping to put through college, has been deceiving them, unprincipled Monica has persuaded him to withdraw the Boys' Club funds from the bank, marry her, and run away to Florida. The Boys' Club funds are substantial, since the club has been given five thousand dollars by Mr. Van Vleck, publisher of the *Banner,* to build a gymnasium.

Lonny, Monica, and a friend leave for Florida in Lonny's old jalopy. Rosemary and Bill are terribly worried about Lonny's disappearance, but during the evening of the flight—which takes weeks of audience time to unfold—their differing attitudes toward the boy cause problems in their relationship. Rosemary is sure that their faith and trust have made Lonny a good boy; Bill feels they should give up on him.

Lonny, repenting what he has done, drives on and on through a blizzard, refusing to stop for the night. Eventually, on the pretext of asking directions, he goes into a drugstore, where he buys an envelope and a stamp, and mails the Boys' Club money back to the bank. Then, in the middle of the night, his two companions asleep, he turns the car around and heads back toward Springdale to face the music. When Monica realizes that they are no longer on their way to Florida she grabs the wheel; the car skids into a telephone pole.

When Rosemary and Bill are notified that the three young people are in the hospital, they rush there. In her delirium, Monica reveals that Lonny has taken the Boys' Club money. Bill is immediately outraged; Rosemary refuses to believe Lonny capable of such a thing. Before the truth about the return of the money comes out, the Robertses' marital problem is exacerbated. Then a trooper arrives to charge Lonny with killing a man in a hit-and-run accident shortly before his own crash.

Eventually Rosemary is able to prove Lonny's innocence—he was buying gas at ten minutes past two, forty miles from the location of the hit-and-run accident that took place at two o'clock—and he is freed, only to find that Monica has died of her injuries.

Lonny feels he must get away from Springdale and try to forget. The rift in the Robertses' marriage is repaired when a new neighbor, Diane Thompson, points out to Rosemary that she has given Lonny too large a place in her life, trying to use him as a substitute for the baby she lost. Rosemary sees the wisdom of this immediately: of course she cannot make someone who is not her own child such an important part of her concern. She and Bill, reconciled, are rapturous at the prospect of having their house to themselves once more. Diane Thompson suggests that they celebrate their new-found freedom by taking a week's vacation in New York with her.

Off they go for a week of fun at the Hotel Dalton. Mrs. Thompson invites them to a dinner being given in her honor as founder of a group called the Little Mothers that "worked with" teen-agers. Rosemary is impressed by the number and status of Diane Thompson's friends.

By this time Rosemary considers Diane a close friend, but there is still something a bit odd about Mrs. Thompson. Strange little things do keep happening. Telegrams arrive that make her turn pale. She is not in when Rosemary telephones her, though she has been seen to enter the hotel. A rough-looking fellow accosts her and insists that her name is Goldie. On the last day of the New York vacation, Diane has arranged to meet Bill and Rosemary in the hotel lobby so they can return to Springdale together, but instead is discovered sobbing hysterically in her room. She insists that they leave without her.

But the main change brought about in the lives of the Robertses by their week in New York is that Mr. Wilson, an ad agency man for whom Bill once worked, many, many scripts ago, asks him to write a series of articles for a national magazine. Not only will Bill be well paid, but he will be doing enormous good for the youth of America, for this is to be an exposé of narcotics and the terrible harm they do to young people. Bill will work closely with the Narcotics Squad (presumably part of the FBI, since they operate all over the country) and will be with them as they search out and arrest the underworld leaders responsible for drug use.

This is dangerous work. Threatening phone calls begin as

soon as Bill and Rosemary return to Springdale. The gangsters apparently want Bill to give up his investigation, but he won't even consider it. Back and forth he goes, to New York and Chicago, increasingly dedicated to his intensive study of the narcotics problem.

He is aided in this undertaking by a beautiful young researcher, Mercy Ainsworth, of whom Rosemary is immediately jealous. And why wouldn't she be? Bill's work is secret; he is not supposed to discuss it even with his wife. He is always off swapping drug statistics and case histories with Mercy over lunch in New York while Rosemary droops at home.

Fortunately she has some companionship from the increasingly mysterious Diane Thompson. And then Diane's brother Ray arrives with his little girl, age five. Rosemary volunteers to take care of adorable little Betsy during the day, since Diane works and Ray is, he says, looking for a job.

Rosemary and Bill, too, on his flying visits, find Ray perfectly charming, though Bill somewhat resents the constant presence of Betsy. However, the audience knows that Ray is not the delightful companion he appears; alone with Diane, he is unquestionably a bad egg. He knows things that he holds over Diane to keep her in line; he twists her arm when annoyed. And from phone calls he makes to New York we learn that he is actually in Springdale only to spy on Bill Roberts. Ray gives information that enables the big drug pusher, Smitty, to elude the Narcotics Squad's pursuit in Chicago, to everyone's mystified consternation.

So here we have potent stuff brewing. Evidently Ray is part of the drug ring Bill is pursuing. Threats have been made against Bill to Rosemary. Threats against Rosemary have been made to Bill. Rosemary is deep in her problem of making someone else's child her own. She is also miserably jealous of Mercy Ainsworth. Mr. Van Vleck (the publisher, remember) is deeply disturbed by Bill's neglect of the *Banner,* which is no longer the outstanding newspaper Bill had made it. Diane Thompson wants her brother to leave town. His underworld employers have told him to get a job as test pilot at the local helicopter plant and to make contact with some people in Portland, Maine, obviously with drug deliveries in mind. Can the mysterious Diane be an addict? Is her name really Goldie? Is Ray perhaps not her brother but her husband? Or is Ray in love with Rosemary? Will the gangsters make an attempt on Bill's life? On Rosemary's? Is little Betsy's toy panda, which has a zipper in its back, going to be used as a hiding place for heroin?

At this point, suddenly, most of these problems and questions are abruptly dropped. Presumably the decision has been made to start drawing the story to a close. But the wrap-up, well-intentioned though it may be, is unsatisfying.

Bill decides that Springdale is too small a place, the *Banner* too small a vocation, for a man of his talents. He is anxious to dedicate his life to bigger things, presumably having some relation to writing, to narcotics, and perhaps to Mercy Ainsworth. For all the previous questions the audience has been wondering about, a new one is substituted: What should Rosemary's attitude toward her husband's decision be?

Lonny Cisare returns from New York. In the month he has been away, he has matured. All his troubles are behind him now, part of the fever of Monica that has burned itself out in his blood. Now he knows happiness is not to be found in the impersonal big city. He has accepted the invitation of an adoring high school girl, Betty Gray, to the senior prom, and he realizes that she is the girl for him. Lonny and Betty go to visit Lonny's sister's new baby, which inspires them to plan marriage.

Bill Roberts, at Mercy's urging, decides to move to New York. He quits his job on the *Banner*. Rosemary says that wherever Bill wants to go, whatever he wants to do, is all right with her. Larry, the assistant editor who is married to Lonny's sister, warns Bill that Mr. Van Vleck won't keep the *Banner* going if Bill isn't there to run it, but Bill is adamant. So Larry buys out Van Vleck with money nobody ever suspected he had, deciding to run the paper himself, with Lonny as his partner. Lonny is delighted by this turn of events. Determined to become a great journalist, he is now in a position to marry Betty.

Rosemary has been showing the Roberts house to prospective tenants preparatory to moving to New York. When she tells Bill that she has found a couple who want to rent the place, however, he balks. He has, in fact, completely reversed his position. He feels that he is being pushed out of both home and job and decides that he will not, after all, go to New York.

The Lonny-Betty marriage takes place in Rosemary's house, with the reception at Betty's parents' home across the street. Rosemary and Mrs. Gray have been living across the street from each other all this time but, interestingly enough, have never met before. The wedding is a great success. After all, as various characters ask, isn't it wonderful to marry when you're so in love and can spend your youth together and even have your children while you're still young enough to enjoy them?

Lonny and Betty decide to spend their honeymoon in their own little house, which Rosemary and Anna have helped Lonny get ready as a surprise for Betty, including a complete dinner for the newlyweds in the refrigerator.

Now that the idea of moving has been abandoned, Rosemary and Bill spend the evening of the wedding at home. True, Bill has no job and no plans for the future, but they are happy because they are together and in Springdale. Suddenly Mercy arrives to try to argue Bill into changing his decision and moving to New York after all. Rosemary, realizing that this is a turning point in her married life, summons all her strength and leaves Bill alone to decide her fate with Mercy.

Rosemary pays a call on her mother and stepfather. They know every detail of the situation and sympathize with her, but they wonder if she should not fight harder to save her marriage. She tells them that the decision must be Bill's and Bill's alone. Then Bill appears. He has told Mercy that he can't go to New York. He has made it clear to her that he must spend his life in Springdale because that is what Rosemary wants, and being Rosemary's husband is the most important thing in life to him. He'll take no chances with that.

Next day a happy Rosemary goes to tell Larry that Bill would like nothing better than his job as editor of the *Banner* again.

Larry, no writer, has been pining for Bill's help; he promises Rosemary he'll never let Bill guess that the suggestion came from her and promptly offers Bill the third equal partnership in the *Banner*. Everybody's happiness is complete—except for that portion of the audience that may still be wondering when the gangsters are going to try to kill Rosemary, and whether the friendly Diane Thompson is really a heroin addict with a sinister past.

Helen Trent, who had set out so long before to prove that romance can exist after thirty-five, played her final love scene in 1960. If she was still unmarried when last heard from, at least she was engaged to a strong man who would presumably put an end to her perennial search.

Helen, standing on a terrace, the sea behind her, is talking to senatorial candidate John Cole. Romantic string music underlies the scene.

JOHN: Helen, I love you.

HELEN [*laughing*]: Oh, John, you say it like a campaign slogan.

JOHN: I've got to. Helen, you drive me crazy. I'm as sure as that I stand here that as long as I know you I'll be fighting the men off—men you insist on being nice to without *any* idea that every one of them has an ulterior motive.

HELEN: John, that's absurd!

JOHN: It's the truth, Helen. You're *dynamite*! But you won't face it. You've got a little-girl attitude that you can walk through life with men making passes all around you but nothing can ever happen. Well, you've got to grow up someday. Maybe I'm the guy to show you how.

HELEN: Maybe you are, John.

JOHN: But if I do, I'll be tough. I'll knock the first man down who looks at you!

HELEN [*ecstatically*]: Oh, will you!

JOHN [*chuckling*]: Well, you scrappy little wench you. [*Change of tone.*] Helen . . . will you marry me?

HELEN [*startled*]: Oh, John?

JOHN: Now don't say it's a surprise. You've had your hooks into me for months. I won't ask you to set a date; I'm going to win this election bare-knuckled first.

HELEN: Oh, you *will* win it, John. You'll win it because you have everything it takes . . . courage and honesty, toughness and ideals. [*Hushed.*] Oh, John, I love you so much.

JOHN: Will you wait . . . six months?

HELEN: Oh, yes. I'll wait six months. Darling I'll wait—

JOHN [*interupting*]: Not *forever,* Helen. [*Whispering*] Not unless you're sure.

HELEN: I'm sure now, John . . . very sure.

MUSIC: *"Love, Here Is My Heart"* up full, then under for

ANNOUNCER: With this broadcast we bring to an end the present series in *The Romance of Helen Trent.*

The very last of the radio soaps to go off the air abandoned their audiences during Thanksgiving week, 1960. From a summary of their concluding story lines, it is clear that a number of long-standing major problems were shuffled to a hasty conclusion; perhaps the listeners were disposed to forgive this arbitrary foreshortening of events, since it seemed to promise all the soap characters a happy, if inaudible, future. CBS described the last week in the lives of its last four soaps this way:

Right to Happiness: Now that Dick Braden has been paroled from prison and his parents have become reconciled, the Braden family is united again. Grace has assured Skip that he is the only boy in her life, and Lee's court case has come to a satisfactory close, even though the missing witness has not been found. Carolyn and Lee now face the future with assurance, the events of the past few weeks having brought them closer than ever together.

Ma Perkins: Charlie Lindstrom has accepted a job in the East. He and Mary are taking leave of Ma Perkins and Rushville Center. On Thanksgiving Day, the entire family is gathered at Ma's house. Ma Perkins herself sees happiness ahead, primarily because Anushka and her grandson, Junior, will be married next month.

Young Dr. Malone: During a hospital board meeting, Judge Allen attempts to force Dr. Ted Mason to resign as director of the clinic, a post formerly held by Dr. Jerry Malone. The latter refuses to accept the board's offer to reinstate him. Ted's first reaction is that of relief, but, after Molly West makes him see the truth about his untenable position, he calls on Jerry, asking him to go back to his old job. When Mason tells him that he is leaving immediately for a destination somewhere out West where he can think out his many problems, Jerry agrees to return as head of the clinic.

Meanwhile, plans for the wedding between Scotty and Jill proceed, despite the open antagonism of his possessive mother. In a last effort to effect a reconciliation, Dr. Malone calls upon Mrs. Scott and makes her realize that her son's love must be shared. Finally, she tells her son and future daughter-in-law that she will attend the wedding after all.

Second Mrs. Burton: Terry realizes that Mother has gotten herself into a trap by agreeing to take her young artist-protégé, Fenno, to Paris. Arranging to send Fenno abroad with a young friend in her place, Terry gets Mother out of that predicament, much to the relief of the rest of the family.

As for Mother Burton, she now concentrates all her energies into preparing for an ambitious Christmas bazaar. Thanksgiving Day dinner at her house is highlighted by the return of Lew and Marcia from their Caribbean vacation.

Deep in the very nature of soaps is the implied promise that they will last forever, and now that promise had been broken. The world of radio soap was no more. All those towns—Beechwood, Rushville Center, Simpsonville, Springdale—all had vanished without a trace. Their inhabitants, whose private lives the listeners knew so intimately, whose fears and joys and hopes they had so long shared, those people of Soapland whose relation to the audience was in some ways more like possession than like friendship, all were gone. They had entered the realm of folklore.

SOAPS RISE AGAIN

§

[*Silence. Close-up of radio in trash can. Pull back to reveal* MADELEINE *and* DAVID *sitting before their silent typewriters. It is still dark outside. Despair. Suddenly a loud ring of the telephone breaks the stillness.*]

DAVID [*removing his eyeshade*]: What's that?

MADELEINE: The telephone.

DAVID: Who is it?

MADELEINE: It may be Frank.

DAVID: Who's Frank?

MADELEINE: You know Frank. Ellen's brother who was just acquitted by the jury after that trial in which he was unjustly accused of murdering his sister-in-law, Maureen, who, it turns out, was not dead after all, just in New York seeing old Dr. Jonathan about her bad ankle which has never been quite right since the accident when she—

DAVID: Yes, I know Frank. Answer the phone.

MADELEINE: Hello . . . Yes? . . . Oh, good, good? . . . You will? . . . You're coming up right now to hook it up? That's fine . . . How's Ellen? . . . Good. See you in a minute . . . Thank you . . . Goodbye.

DAVID: Who was that?

MADELEINE: Frank. You know, Ellen's brother who was just acquitted—

DAVID: Yes, I know Frank. Why is he coming here?

MADELEINE: You were listening, weren't you, you sly puss? It was supposed to be a surprise. Frank is now a television salesman and he's coming up to deliver the television set I just bought.

DAVID: What's a television set?

MADELEINE: You *are* an innocent. It's something we need in order to write the next chapter.

As the radio soaps slowly and sadly faded away, to the accompanying sighs of their loyal audiences, a spattering of applause was heard from those critics who had never understood how any sane, sensible person could actually be listening to all that trash. Some of them anticipated the passing of the soap era as a victory for the American woman. She was now reaching, they said, a plane of education and maturity where soap opera could no longer satisfy her desire for art, culture, and reliable data about the gritty, complicated, real world she lived in and was now eager to face.

There was, of course, the possibility that soap opera would not quite die, that it would simply transmigrate. Perhaps it would live again on television, to continue performing its secondary task of bedeviling the nation's husbands and critics, and its primary one of maintaining American womanhood in a state of unwholesome addiction.

But that possibility was widely discounted. True, attempts were being made to transfer the old wine to the new bottles. As early as 1946 a single episode of *Big Sister* had been televised, and a full-scale daytime serial, *A Woman to Remember*, was tried out in 1947; but these experiments were doomed to failure. Indeed, *A Woman to Remember* bore out the prediction admirably, as it promptly collapsed. Hundreds of wits must have suggested that a more appropriate title might have been *A Woman to Forget*.

In 1950 CBS with much fanfare introduced an ambitious experiment, *The First Hundred Years*. This title was intended to suggest that the program would chronicle a marriage, the first hundred years of which are proverbially the hardest. When the program left the air, critics gleefully pointed out that the title had missed its mark by ninety-nine years.

Things were going just as everyone who deplored soap opera had hoped they would, and they had common sense and economics on their side. After all, how could soap opera ever be successful on television? The obstacles in its way were immense and most likely insurmountable.

In the first place there was cost. Producing a serial for television was immeasurably more complicated than producing one for radio. *The First Hundred Years* needed a production crew of twenty-seven, and that wasn't counting actors, product demonstrators, organist, and announcer. The weekly cost of producing a fifteen-minute daily television serial was $8650, as opposed to $3500 for a radio serial. How, then, could a television soap ever be profitable?

Production problems, too, were multitudinous. Places and people were now right there on the television screen, so sets had to be built and actors appropriately costumed. All props mentioned in the script actually had to be on the set. No invisible Christmas presents would ever evoke cries of delight on television soap opera; no empty cups of coffee could be comfortingly poured and gratefully imbibed. And actors would no longer read their lines from mimeographed sheets as they had in the simple days of radio. Four and a half hours of rehearsal were necessary for each fifteen-minute episode—and how were the actors to memorize all those lines? Clearly it was beyond human capacity.

The visibility of everything could be expected to pose problems for the writer as well. No longer could the young husband and wife blithely jump into their car to discuss the joys of marriage as they drove to the station, since there would be no car, and no station either. Nor could they so conveniently bid each other a tearful farewell on the pier or poke their way with such ease through a haunted mansion.

And as for the satisfaction of the audience's deepest wishes, television soap opera could never succeed in purveying the imaginary world the soap fan craved and was accustomed to. The housewife was in the habit of identifying closely with a heroine, a heroine whose appearance she could imagine to suit herself. If the heroine was said to be ideally beautiful, an appropriate vision of ideal beauty could float before the listener's eyes without conflicting in the slightest detail with

(ABOVE) Mary Stuart, Queen of Soaps. She
has played Joanne on *Search for Tomorrow*,
the oldest extant TV soap, since its premiere September 3, 1951.

(RIGHT) Audrey Peters, Vanessa Sterling
on *Love of Life*, is congratulated by Larry
Auerbach, who has directed the show for
twenty-two years.

James Pritchett and Elizabeth Hubbard with some of *The Doctors'* ten years of scripts.

Helen Wagner and Don McLaughlin, Nancy and Chris Hughes of *As the World Turns*, with fan mail.

The director in the control room watches the show on monitors (TOP LEFT); actors are positioned on the sets (TOP RIGHT AND CENTER LEFT); two important aids, the teleprompter and the stopwatch (CENTER); the organist makes notes in his script (CENTER RIGHT); the actors in the makeup room (BOTTOM LEFT); and the show on the air (BOTTOM RIGHT).

David Rounds as Philip Holden, with Ron Tomme as Bruce
Sterling, and Audrey Peters as Vanessa, on the set of *Love
of Life* in 1963.

Another World, created by Irna Phillips and now almost ten years on the air, in a recent dress rehearsal.

the quite different fantasy personage floating before the eyes of the woman at the radio next door. The heroine's clothes, too, not to mention her husband, her lovers, and her decor, would be perfectly suited to the listening audience's taste. How could any real live persons satisfy such exigencies? How could mere mortals exert the necessary appeal over so broad a spectrum?

The critics had the best of the argument at first. Nothing was working for television soaps. Programs were put on the air, tinkered with, withdrawn. Various theories were advanced to explain their lack of success. Perhaps there were too many career-girl heroines? Perhaps too much or too little was happening? Maybe the TV soaps were too much like those of radio or too different? They certainly were expensive to produce.

To counter this last drawback, CBS experimented with a new length, the half hour. Production costs for producing one half-hour episode were far lower than those of two fifteen-minute episodes for different shows, and the amount of time available to be sold for commercials was unchanged. Lengthening the soap episode therefore made sense for the network, and it turned out to have a delightfully unexpected side effect as well: viewers approved the new length.

Persistence eventually won out. By trial and error the networks discovered that soap opera could not only live but flourish in the new medium. The critics were confounded, the network people were jubilant, and the audience was happy. Now they had soap opera on their new television sets as well as on their old radios, and sometimes the same show, using exactly the same script, on both. Now when the old favorites of radio glided away one by one into the ether, their audiences would not be entirely bereft; they would still be able to turn a dial that provided entry into the magical world of soap.

The very early television soaps were almost indistinguishable from radio programs. The visual aspect of the new medium turned out not to be as crucial as had been feared. After all, soaps had always been largely domestic; it was not at all impossible to limit most of the action to easily built indoor sets. And television cameras did not force the soaps to provide more dramatic action than before, since it turned out that a great portion of the audience was not watching the screen anyway; they simply left the set on and went about their usual round of household activities, exactly like a radio soap audience. Early television soaps even kept the announcer, that useful intruder who was so helpful in commenting on the action and directing the attention of the audience to the most fruitful themes of future interest.

The stories the new soaps told were the same stories radio listeners were accustomed to. In other words, radio and television, far from being rivals for the minds of the audience, had turned out to be allies. All this is plainly evident in the early television soap *Follow Your Heart,* first aired in 1953, as an account of its plot developments will show.

The heroine of *Follow Your Heart,* beautiful Julie Fielding, who is nineteen, lives with her mother and her younger sister, Jocelyn, in Worthington House in Ardmore, on the Main Line. They are rich and fashionable, an old family. They live by tradition and convention in most respects, but the family is oddly constituted in that the parents have been separated for many years and the father continues to live nearby, in a hotel. He does not belong to one of the old local families but runs his own one-man scientific research laboratory.

As the story begins, Mrs. Fielding and her daughters are in a whirl of social activity. Julie is engaged to Harry Phillips, a rich and well-born neighbor, and tonight will be their engagement party. A society reporter comes to interview Julie; there is much talk about what she will wear and when the wedding will be. Mrs. Fielding is ecstatic, Jocelyn is thrilled, but Julie clearly has her doubts. The talk turns to love. It is quickly apparent that Julie wonders if she is doing the right thing in marrying Harry. Of course, she has known him all her life, and she's very fond of him, but "It would be a lot more fun," she muses wistfully, "to be marrying a stranger—somebody I didn't know a thing about—somebody I fell head over heels in love with—madly—frantically in love—"

Julie has strong feelings about marriage, and high hopes that hers will be a success. Marriage, she says, "should be as big as your religion, as strong as what you feel about your country—as deep as what you feel about your parents—as what you know you will feel about your children . . ." But still she doubts. Perhaps Harry is not the right man.

Julie takes her doubts to her father, whom she loves. He, as an estranged husband, is not invited to the engagement party, but they both assume he will give her away when she marries. "Dad," she asks, "how do you know when you're in love?" Fielding has no doubts or conflicts on this point, and thus no difficulty with his daughter's question. "Your heart tells you, kitten," he soothes her. "Just follow your heart."

The promptings of Julie's heart are unclear, however. She and her fiancé, Harry, have a drink together before the engagement party, and argue about Julie's desire to run off to an island. Harry is willing to spend a long honeymoon on an island, but unadventurously prefers to settle down in his hometown.

"We belong here, Julie," he tells her. "We belong here where we've grown up and where we have our roots deep in this soil." Julie still hovers on the brink of disaffection. Certainty has to come from him. "Oh, Harry," she implores, "make me very, very sure."

The first conflict of the show is the question of what kind of love one must have in order to assure successful marriage. Can one marry without love and expect to find happiness?

On the evening of the party all is confusion. The teen-age sister, Jocelyn, rushes upstairs to tell Julie the man has arrived to fix the piano, "and, boy—is he a *dreamboat!*" Will Julie come down and explain what he should do? Down she comes, to encounter a handsome young man playing a haunting melody on the piano. Their eyes meet.

Of course, this is not the piano tuner. That was all a mixup. The young man, whose name turns out to be Peter Davis, has really come because he had an appointment for a job interview with Julie's father, Samuel Tilden Fielding, at five o'clock. He got the address from the phone book, which has been permitted to offer the wrong address ever since the Fieldings separated fifteen years ago.

The two young people are immediately drawn to each other, but by now Peter is late to his appointment with Mr. Fielding. Julie pleads for permission to drive him to her father's hotel, but he refuses. Sturdily independent, he will accept no favors. Already the lines are drawn: they are from different worlds.

"Just forget about me," Peter tells her curtly. "You're engaged to somebody else. Remember?"

JULIE: I remember . . . [*Pause.*] I heard a young man play a song of his own . . . I'll never forget it.

PETER: I'm sorry about that too.

JULIE: Because you let me see inside your—heart—for a minute?

PETER: I've got no business having a heart. I'm too poor. I can't afford a heart.

ANNOUNCER: Maybe it isn't only in storybooks that you suddenly meet the handsome stranger. Maybe he's there, everywhere, all the time, waiting for that fateful moment. And now Julie thinks of her father's advice, "Follow your heart." And she thinks of the stranger, handsome Peter Davis, and of the tune, his tune, playing in her heart. And tonight is Julie's engagement party.

The real piano tuner at last arrives, and turns out to have known Peter as a child. He describes him as poor, without family, but brilliant and talented. Julie, her opinion of Peter reinforced, calls her father and explains the reasons for the missed appointment. As she is imploring him to give Peter a chance, Peter calls on his other phone and is allowed to make a new appointment.

That night Harry slips the engagement ring on Julie's finger, but the audience knows she is thinking of Peter because she has been distrait ever since Peter's theme music sneaked under the song she and Harry were dancing to. Julie stares into space as Harry embraces her, saying, "I'm so happy, Julie. I guess I never really believed you'd have me. I'll do anything to make you happy, Julie. Anything in this world."

Julie does not know what to do about her sudden new feelings. When Harry's mother gives her the family pearls, she accepts them. Perhaps she can put Peter out of her mind and go on as if nothing had happened. But when Julie visits her father she finds he has hired Peter as his assistant at the lab.

Peter says he must be on his way, and Julie insists on driving him home; but when she invites him to dinner he says, "What's the use, Miss Fielding?"

The announcer recognizes Julie's dilemma: "When you suddenly meet a stranger, and your heart tells you he's the one man you've been waiting for all your life—what do you do if you're already engaged to someone else?"

Peter has rented a room in the home of the widow and daughter of his old chemistry teacher, Professor MacKenzie. Georgie MacKenzie, the daughter, is an attractive young bacteriologist employed at the town waterworks. She and Peter share an interest in science, and she invites him to use her dead father's laboratory, which she still maintains. They become fast friends, and Mrs. MacKenzie cooks for and mothers them both.

Peter never confides his nascent feelings about Julie to Georgie. When the subject does turn to Julie, with whom Georgie is slightly acquainted, and Georgie says, "It would be wonderful to look like Julie Fielding and be able to dress like her and live in that big house," Peter replies with no more revealing a statement than "You know you'd ten times rather be you—with a job—than Julie Fielding rattling around in that big lonely house."

Julie tells her father that she wants to break her engagement because she is in love with Peter. Sam protests, "But you don't know a thing about him." Julie argues that she knows how she feels. "I know," she says, "I know I'd come running if he whistles—I know if he held up a hoop I'd—jump through."

Can this be love at first sight? "Yes—really and truly—love at first sight." Love has changed her. She is resolved that "I can learn to be everything he wants me to be. I'll go anywhere he wants me to go. I'll—I'll scrub floors and wash dishes and cook dinners for him." She concludes: "I'll learn to be a woman, not a—a stupid girl." Her father is delighted with her resolve.

Julie goes home and confides the truth about her romantic

situation to her sister. She is going to break off with Harry because she loves Peter. "All I know, Jocey, is that nothing matters except that he's in the world." Jocelyn does not fully approve, but is prepared to stand by Julie whatever comes.

Julie then breaks the news to her mother, but without telling her the whole story. For her mother's benefit she explains that she has decided she cannot marry Harry because she realizes she does not love him. Mrs. Fielding does her utmost to patch things up between Julie and Harry. As she says to Julie, "Maybe you don't love him wildly, passionately, but that kind of love doesn't last—it's friendship that lasts—it's marrying somebody of your own kind who speaks your own language that lasts. In six months what you call love, this so-called enduring passion, is gone—burned out—and then where is a marriage?"

Mrs. Fielding manages to warn Harry that Julie is going to try to break the engagement. She asks him to be understanding, explaining to him that Julie's odd behavior is all the result of her father's influence, and assuring him that Julie will eventually come to her senses. So when Julie tells Harry of her doubts about their relationship he soothes her with "You don't know what love is, darling," and insists that they go along as if nothing had happened.

Julie, unable to break with convention, goes back to her father for encouragement, and gets it. "It takes a lot of honesty and courage to listen to your heart and follow its message," he reminds her. "The thing to remember and hold on to—is the fact that your heart does tell you the truth—with honesty and courage and love, you can't go wrong—"

Mrs. Fielding visits her husband to confer about Julie's problems, and they argue their two theories of love. Mrs. Fielding is still sure she is right about passionate love. As she reminds her husband, "You and I, Sam, lost our heads for a wild passion—and where did it get us? Fighting like cat and dog—I wanted to protect Julie from that." But Sam continues to encourage Julie, going so far as to inform Peter that Julie is trying to break her engagement.

Meanwhile, at the MacKenzies', the Peter-Georgie relationship is intensifying, at least on Georgie's side. Peter nicknames her Redhead, and Georgie says, "Nobody ever called me Redhead but you." "Like it?" Peter inquires. "Uh-huh, I like it when you say it," she answers, adding, "I'd kill anybody else who called me that."

Peter is too dense or too preoccupied to notice this growing adoration, and frequently discusses Julie's problems with Georgie. He tells her that Julie "needs a friend."

Julie is still anxious to break off with Harry and get her life organized on a different basis. She suggests to her father that perhaps she should come live with him. He rejects this plan but counsels Julie that Peter will never "give you a tumble as long as you're engaged to Harry" because Peter is "a square shooter." Julie, determined to straighten things out with Peter, who is still suspicious of her motives, follows him to the local luncheonette. She explains to him that she does not love Harry, but Peter and she disagree about whether or not she should consider herself free.

PETER: And I'd thank you to stop trying to get cozy with me until you get the point settled one way or another.

JULIE: You've got your nerve.

PETER: I've got it . . . because I have to have it.

JULIE: Oh, really! I suppose I'm making myself such a nuisance, throwing myself at your head.

PETER: You can't be that much of a dope.

JULIE: So now I'm a—

PETER: I told you . . . I've never met anyone like you. I could be crazy about you at the drop of a hat—if I let myself.

At this critical juncture Georgie appears to tell Peter she has just been given a raise, but her enthusiasm is dashed by the sight of Julie. The announcer defines the conflict: "And so the triangle develops . . . an old, old story . . . always bitter and always poignant because of the heartbreak it involves for someone. Which of the girls is capable of loving Peter more?"

Julie and Peter recognize that they come from two different worlds, and to Peter this seems an insuperable problem. Georgie, the poor but honest worker, is clearly the suitable girl for him. Yet it is Julie who attracts him. Peter admits to Mr. Fielding that if Julie were free and if he had money, things might be very different. Sam is by now very fond of Peter and encourages him, even though he has recently found out that Peter was once fired from a job "for good and just causes." (Questioned about that, all Peter would say was, "I guess you'll just have to take me on faith—if you want me." Fielding dropped the subject.)

Jocelyn accidentally lets out the truth about Julie's feelings for Peter to the girls' mother, who is horrified. Julie admits, "I think he's wonderful! I think he's the most wonderful person on earth." Mrs. Fielding protests, "Don't tell me you 'love' Peter?" and Julie temporizes. "I don't know," she says. "That's one of the things I want to find out." Mrs. Fielding takes this opportunity to explain that marrying for love is a mistake she herself has made and one she hopes Julie will not repeat. The scene is interrupted by the ringing of the doorbell. Mrs. Fielding, in distress, retires to her room, leaving Julie to answer the bell. The visitor proves to be a sinister fellow looking for Peter Davis, who he claims is an old friend. His name is Nicky Destini, and the audience can tell at a glance that he is a gangster.

Julie, having disclaimed any knowledge of Peter's whereabouts, rushes off to the lab to warn him that a gangster is on his trail. Peter refuses to answer any of her questions about his relationship with Nicky. "You'd better forget that you ever met me," he discourages her. "I told you before that we belonged to different worlds. Now maybe you're getting some idea of what I mean." But Julie refuses to accept defeat. "No!" she insists. "However things look, I know you're not Nicky's kind. He means trouble for you. And he probably has before—without *your* doing anything wrong."

The announcer understands the issues involved. "What are the limits of faith? How long can you go on believing in a man who won't speak a word to clear himself? And yet Julie knows that this is a test. If love is worth anything at all, it must stand the strain of suspicion and doubt and come through stronger than before."

When Peter and Nicky meet, it is clear that they have had a long, intimate, and perhaps criminal association. Peter is surprised to see Nicky alive, having thought him killed in a raid. Nicky explains: "It was curtains for Big Mike . . . and for Spider and for Brown—the yaps. They should have known better than to try to shoot it out with the feds." He tells Peter how he managed to escape and explains that he has been lying low ever since.

Now, however, he has a new boss, and they have a project that involves Peter. Nicky has come, knowing that the Fielding lab has just been given a top-secret government contract, to offer Peter fifty thousand dollars to pass on information about it to his boss. Peter demurs, saying he is through with that kind of thing, but offers to find Nicky another helpful chemist. Nicky is dubious; he can only relay this offer to his boss and return in a few days to let Peter know what the reaction is.

Georgie's love for Peter increases day by day, and her mother, noticing her deepening involvement, has warned her, "Don't let Peter fill your heart." To Peter, Mrs. MacKenzie has gone so far as to say, "Peter—Georgie thinks a lot of you—you know that, don't you?" But Peter, though momentarily troubled, is too much taken up with his choice between deeper involvement with Julie and the possibility of resuming his connection with the underworld to pay much attention.

Confused, Peter sketches the basic outlines of his problem for Sam. He admits that there is a shadow on his life, and that he has no right to a girl like Julie. And yet, what he wants above all is marriage. "It's the most natural thing in the world for a guy to want to raise a family," he explains. "That's what we're here for. You can be the biggest so-called success in the world—engineer, scientist, I don't care what. But if you haven't got a family—the basic thing that everybody wants —you're a bust." Sam suggests that Peter explain everything to Julie and let her decide whether she is willing to trust him, despite whatever dark things may lie in his past. Peter decides to take this advice.

When Peter arrives at the Fielding house, Julie is out for a dinner and theater date with Harry, but Jocelyn entertains Peter while he awaits their return. When Harry and Julie appear Harry's jealousy is aroused by the sight of a rival, and he asserts his rights as fiancé. "We're engaged," he protests. "No," says Julie, "we're *not*." Harry accuses her of jilting him for Peter, and Julie explains that things are not quite as he thinks. Her desire to break their engagement is not simply a rejection of him but a break with her whole past way of life. "All right," she says, "Peter did have something to do with it. But not in the way you think . . . Somehow, meeting him made me realize I couldn't go on for the rest of my life in an eternal atmosphere of cocktail parties. There had to be something different, or life just wasn't worth living."

Peter is naturally delighted to hear this. When he and Julie are alone, he can no longer, despite Nicky and the shadows of the past, resist her. He takes her in his arms.

ANNOUNCER: Can a kiss solve all problems? Can the welling storm of love scatter obstacles to the wind?

PETER: Julie . . . Julie . . .

[*They kiss—long kiss.*]

PETER [*finally*]: My dear one!

JULIE: This is what I've dreamed of . . . for so long. Oh, Peter—[*her head on his shoulder*] And it's happened . . .

PETER [*looking up*]: I want to hold you like this for as long as those stars up there swing around the world.

They begin to discuss marriage. But their problems are far from solved: at the first mention of Julie's trust fund, Peter retreats in panic. She is too rich; the gap can never be bridged. When he leaves, he kisses her valedictorily on the forehead.

Julie is aware that if their relationship is to succeed she must make herself over into a person Peter can respect. She must break away from the life of the idle rich, and she vows to do so. Though she cannot make her mother understand this, despite repeated efforts, she does eventually convince Harry. So impressed is he by the change in Julie that he resigns all proprietary rights over her and, abandoning any romantic aspirations, becomes her friendly champion in her continuing conflict with her mother over Peter Davis.

He tries to explain to Mrs. Fielding that Julie really intends to "make something of her life" and that "this Peter Davis is a pretty lucky guy." "Not too lucky yet," Julie protests modestly, "but I mean to see he is before I get through." Mrs. Fielding, having lost Harry as ally and protégé, says, "I'm leaving you two together to talk this nonsense." Julie, as her mother departs, happily announces: "I like talking to Harry now. Suddenly everything's right between us."

Peter, still fearing that he and Julie are too far apart ever to settle their differences, continues his friendship with Georgie, but his nightmares reveal that he is deep in conflict about what role Julie will play in his life.

When Julie asks Peter to meet her at "their" place, he goes. She has great news for him, she announces. She has begun to change her life so that she can be worthy of him. She has a job.

Perhaps all their problems are solved? No, far from it. Rather, it is back to square one in the two-different-worlds game. Julie has volunteered to help out at the country club library. Peter has nothing but contempt for this dilettantish, rich-girl approach to the realities of work, and laughs at her. She furiously slaps him. As they glare at each other the announcer observes: "The rocket explodes in the sky. Sparks fly . . . which must fall to earth somewhere . . . The last time these two met here, it ended in an embrace. But not tonight. The gulf is too wide . . . and neither would dream of moving a step nearer to the edge . . . Is it all over, then, in this tempestuous love affair that hardly got started? Or is Julie the type of girl who never gives up . . . once her goal is set?"

Nicky returns to tell Peter the boss won't take no for an answer. Peter must spy on Sam Fielding's government research. Peter explains that his unwillingness is not the only obstacle to his cooperation; the FBI will run a thorough check on him before the government project can begin, and he is bound to fail. The FBI will discover that he was fired from his previous job on suspicion of stealing narcotics. Nicky is sure the boss will figure out a solution.

Georgie is far happier now that Peter is no longer seeing Julie and has assured her that he and Julie were never meant for each other. So well disposed toward Julie is she now, in fact, that she helps her find a job at the waterworks as a file clerk. Georgie's mother, however, is aware that Peter's feeling for Julie goes far deeper than Georgie will admit.

Peter, even though he has abandoned his hopes for love with Julie, is still anxious to avoid entanglement with Nicky. He has decided that the only way to avoid working for Nicky and his boss is to disappear. He tells Georgie he may soon be leaving town. She believes he has been offered a better job elsewhere and mentions this to Julie at the waterworks.

Desperate at the prospect of abandonment, Julie drops her filing to rush to the lab and confront Peter. He admits that he plans to leave town, explaining that he is in danger and must go into hiding. Julie announces that wherever he goes, she will go. She loves him.

JULIE: Are you trying to scare me, Peter? I'm not scared. I'm going where you're going. I belong to you. I'm yours, Peter—you can't get rid of me.

PETER: You crazy, precious idiot! Listen to me—I'm trying to tell you the truth. This wouldn't be any life for you, Julie. Hunted—running for cover. Never sure when I go out that I'll come home alive. Julie, this isn't for you.

JULIE: I'm not afraid of any kind of a life—if you're in it, Peter. Not for a moment!

Peter can't resist Julie's courageous importunity. "I don't want anything but to be with you, Peter," she insists, "till death us shall part. That's all I want." He moves toward her, slowly at first, and then in a rush to take her in his arms. The music comes up as they kiss, and the announcer discusses the implications of their decision. "If stars can escape from their magnetic fields . . . perhaps a boy and girl have a chance to escape their destiny." The shot dissolves to Julie and Peter still in their embrace, and the announcer continues: "Julie and Peter . . . from every social and practical aspect so unsuited for each other . . . What chance have they got for happiness? How can they help but make out of their lives together what Julie has called un unholy mess? . . . Yet—wouldn't you gladly change places with either of them? For in their wild, tempestuous love there is more of the full richness of life than most of us are given to know . . ."

Peter and Julie plan to marry and disappear into the West together; Julie will wait for Peter to let her know when they will leave. Peter is so happy now that things are right between him and Julie that he decides to take Georgie out on the town for a celebration. As they dine and dance, Georgie, naturally enough, mistakes the signs of Peter's happiness for an increasing interest in her. This misunderstanding persists for some time, and is often discussed by Georgie's mother and a nice young admirer of Georgie's, Bob Randall. Both of them well know that Georgie is deceiving herself and will be hurt, and they are ready to stand by her when the inevitable rejection comes.

Meanwhile, Julie and Peter are planning their future together. They meet often at "their" place. "Peter—I love you!" says Julie. "I'll love you always, Julie," Peter promises. "You're somebody to work for, to live for, to die for." Julie protests, "Don't say that, darling." "I mean it," he answers. "You're worth every sacrifice a man could possibly make."

Finally even Georgie can no longer blind herself to what is going on, and she forces Peter to tell her what his true feelings are for her.

GEORGIE: Peter, say it. I want to know the truth.

PETER: I don't have to say it. You *know.* Don't you? [*Georgie nods and drops her eyes. Peter puts his hand over hers.*] Don't be too upset, little Redhead. These things happen. They aren't anyone's fault . . . Smile for me. [*Georgie smiles with an effort.*] That's my girl.

GEORGIE: I'm going to miss you so.

PETER: No you won't. I'm only one guy in the world.

GEORGIE: The only one for me.

PETER: No sad songs, Georgie. The best of friends must part. And that's the way I'll always think of you.

Peter and Julie have been waiting for word from the FBI; the logical time to leave for the West would be when Peter could no longer work at the lab. But when word comes it is the surprising news that Peter has been cleared. At last the audience gets a clear explanation of Peter's past connection with the underworld: Peter is summoned to meet with Sid

Hemicker, an old friend, who admits he personally arranged Peter's FBI clearance. As Sid says, "I'm a federal agent, and it's my job to break up one of the dirtiest rackets that ever operated in this country." In this he asks for Peter's help. "You did an outstanding job for us as a civilian agent," he says. Now Peter is needed even more—to help Sid put Nicky and his boss behind bars. Peter explains that he wants to leave town to find happiness in the West with Julie. Sid argues, "You thought that narcotics racket Nicky was in was dirty business. Brother, you should know what he's up to now." "I know enough," Peter admits. "He wants the formulas on this top-secret project at the Fielding lab." But Sid knows more. "He wants them," he informs Peter, "or at least his boss wants them . . . for sale to a foreign government."

Sid Hemicker knows what the top-secret project is, though Peter has not yet been told. He explains that if Nicky's gang can get enough information about it, they may bring death to millions of people. Only Peter is in a position to defeat their diabolical plan. But Sid leaves Peter free to decide. "I want you to see with your own eyes what the scum of the earth is up to," he says. "After that, we can talk again, and I promise you, if you still want out . . . the door will be open."

The announcer takes all this very seriously. "Peter has known the crack government agent Sid Hemicker for a long time, and he's never known him to be emotional or excited . . . Yet, in the casual words Sid has just spoken, Peter has caught an undertone of unspeakable horror which makes him uneasy . . . Perhaps, by narrowing down his horizon to just himself and Julie, Peter has withdrawn too far from life. For surely a horror which threatens a hundred and fifty million people must threaten both of them as well . . ."

Peter explains the new situation to Julie, postponing their flight until after he hears what the government project is and can make a decision about what to do. He explains his problem guardedly, but clearly enough to give her some idea of his dilemma. Will he stay on at the lab, or will they run away together? "I'm in a spot, Julie," he tells her. "The same kind of spot that a lot of guys were in during the war . . . You're doing important work and you're not allowed to talk about it. My commanding officer is trying to sign me up for another hitch."

Julie is impressed. "I never realized before what terrible danger you're in," she exclaims. Peter holds her close, kissing her hair. "I couldn't talk before," he says. "But now it's different . . . We're going to be together for the rest of our lives, and you've got to know something."

Now the Georgie-triangle conflict has been resolved and the two-different-worlds problem forgotten. Audience interest must center on Peter's decision: should he seek personal happiness with Julie by running away with her to the West, or is it his duty to remain at the lab because of his obligation to the FBI and humanity in general?

Now Nicky's boss, Alfred Lampier, enters the story. He is a young, suave, handsome fellow with a look of evil in his eyes. His decadence is made clear in a conversation with Nicky about massage. "You don't understand the pleasure of pain, Nicky," he says. "Carl inflicts such exquisite pain." Lampier has decided to accompany Nicky when he returns to Ardmore, to "see what brains can do to make Peter Davis change his mind."

Lampier is, in fact, so clever and has such plausible charm that he is able to introduce himself to Julie and win her confidence immediately. On the pretext that his car has broken down in front of the Fieldings' house, he is admitted to make a phone call. He stays on to charm Mrs. Fielding completely, and is soon deep in intimate talk with Julie.

He tells her that he is the owner of a number of properties out West, places that would be ideal, in their beauty and isolation, for honeymoon couples, or perhaps for people looking for a place to hide. Does she by any chance know of anyone who might be interested in a job as caretaker at one of these retreats? Julie is struck by the appropriateness of this suggestion to her own situation. She admits to knowing a young research chemist who might be interested in just such a position. On further urging, she breaks down and confides to the sympathetic stranger that she and her fiancé are planning to leave town because wicked people are trying to induce him to break the law. Lampier takes an interest, and asks Julie to introduce him to her young man.

Lampier finds himself strongly attracted to Julie and discusses her with Nicky. "A *very* beautiful girl," he suggests. "It's stirred up something in me. Too bad Davis is in the picture. But he's expendable." He continues his reverie: "She'll make a beautiful widow. Or it might even happen before that." Nicky, struck by Lampier's reaction, says, "Never seen you go for a dame before."

Julie tells Peter about Lampier's convenient offer of a refuge for them. He should know by that night, he says, whether they will be going West or not. He does not explain to her that he is about to see Dr. Jacob Grauman, who has come from Washington to explain the top-secret project to Peter and Sam Fielding. Only when he knows what that project entails can he make the decision Sid Hemicker demands. "Peter, darling," Julie begs, as he leaves her, "do what's right . . . But do what's right for us, too. Goodbye, Peter . . . And my love goes with you . . ."

Georgie, trying to recover from her love for Peter, explains to her mother that she knows she will be able to put Peter out of her mind once he has left town. But Peter, now unsure what his future holds, tells the MacKenzies that he may not be leaving after all.

Dr. Jacob Grauman, eminent bacteriologist and head of the entire Top Secret Bacillus Y Project, is of German birth and speaks with an accent. He sets up a movie projector, a screen, and a gooseneck lamp. This done, he introduces the subject. "Gentlemen," he soberly explains, "this is what the enemy intends to do to us. This is the material with which they will wipe human existence out of our country if there is another war." He can't reveal all he knows, of course. "I can tell you very little . . . Secrets must be preserved. But I can say that our agents smuggled this out from another country . . . where years of scientific research have been lavished on this killer."

Sam asks what the films consist of. "They too were smuggled out," Grauman replies. "They are studies of the cellular composition of bacillus Y. Now gentlemen, our problem—in simple language—is this: We must find an antidote for bacillus Y. We must find a chemical, so if the germ bomb is ever dropped on this country, we are prepared to counteract the death and destruction that will result." Bacillus Y is, it appears, the greatest scourge the world has ever known. "There is no escape from bacillus Y. To believe that is to live in a world of dreams . . . Bacillus Y has a new self-generating power unknown formerly to science. Its cells can go on multiplying endlessly. They will spread out into every corner of our country, until there are no more human bodies left to kill . . ."

To prove his point, Grauman then shows Sam and Peter a film of the deadly superbacillus in action. The script explains that "the film selected should show, if possible, a cell multiplying into hundreds of other cells. The screen should be covered with wriggling, horrible things."

The demonstration over, the announcer sums up Peter's problem: "Where can you go when there's no escape? All that's left is to stay and fight . . . For Peter the fight means much more than to find an antidote for bacillus Y. There's his own personal fight for happiness with Julie . . . He must stay now. That much is certain. There's no escape to the West, for all corners of the land are drawn into one spot—the spot where the bomb may strike . . . But marrying Julie now is something else again. For danger threatens him as never before—and how can he expose Julie to that?"

Julie, while she waits for word from Peter as to what his decision will be, goes to visit Lampier at his hotel. She explains that Peter is doing some hard thinking about whether to go West with her or remain at the lab to work on an important project.

Meanwhile, Peter meets Sid Hemicker in the park, and announces that he has decided to stay. Sid congratulates him on having made the right choice, and they plan their operation.

SID: Nicky'll find out before too long that you're still working at the lab. He'll be around for any dope that you can smuggle out. We'll provide you with the material.

PETER: Phonied up . . .

SID: Of course.

PETER: And how long do you think it'll take them to tumble to that little game?

SID: Months . . . maybe less. We'll just have to gamble that we get enough time.

PETER: What are you after?

SID: A complete roundup of Nicky's gang . . . especially the brains at the top . . . this guy that Nicky calls the boss.

PETER: But suppose there isn't time. Suppose they tumble to our game before you find out who the boss is . . .

SID: That's a calculated risk.

PETER: And I'm the expendable—Okay, I'm not complaining. I'll take it if I have to . . . But there's somebody I want protected."

Peter tells Julie he has decided to stay on at the lab; their marriage and flight must be postponed. Julie tells Lampier that Peter is staying on, but promises to call on him if she ever needs help.

Alf Lampier cannot at first understand Peter's change of plan. Why has he decided to forgo his elopement to stay and work for the gang? After long thought he concludes that Peter's decision is based on a desire to make huge sums of money to lavish on the girl he loves. Clearly, Lampier has his blind spots.

But at the same time he has been clever enough to forge a friendship with Mrs. Fielding. She has even begun to look upon him as a possibly suitable match for Julie, and confides all her misgivings about Julie's relationship with Peter. Lampier convinces Mrs. Fielding that she should take a much stronger line with Julie in future; that she should resolutely oppose Julie's marriage to Peter. Then he returns to New York to await developments.

As the announcer explains it, "Lampier, an emperor of evil, has laid the basis for a split between mother and daughter. He has no clear view of what the end will be, but he hopes by this mischief to drive them apart—to break up the unity that has begun to exist between them. Perhaps Julie, isolated, hostile, and bitter toward her mother, will fall an easier victim to him someday . . ."

The envisioned split between mother and daughter takes place, and Julie leaves home. She ends up renting a room from Mrs. MacKenzie, much to Georgie's jealous disapproval. Mrs. MacKenzie realizes that Georgie's resentment of Julie is based on a resurgence of her unrealistic attachment to Peter, and makes it clear that Georgie must learn to accept the truth about Peter's love for Julie.

Mrs. Fielding, once Julie has left home, repents and tries to enlist Mr. Fielding in the attempt to get her back. "I'll do anything to get her back," she says. "I'll get down on my knees and apologize if she wants." Sam sympathizes, but can't help admiring Julie's newfound independence.

At the lab, the top-secret project gets under way. Sam and Peter spend days measuring, testing, experimenting.

PETER: Do you think there's a chance it could break the flask?

SAM: I doubt it. That's special glass, reinforced to steel temper . . . But there's a chance of anything. All right, Pete . . . to your station.

PETER [*uneasily*]: Let me take the observations.

SAM: Certainly not.

PETER: If there are burns . . . I've got a better chance of recovery, Mr. Fielding.

SAM: Pete, you'll do exactly what you're told . . . Now get to your station.

Peter reports to Sid on how the work is progressing. Sid, in turn, tells Peter that the FBI has been unable to trace Nicky to his meetings with the boss. "Each time he reports to his boss he goes through the most elaborate shake-off procedure we've ever run across," he admits. Then Sid presents Peter with the falsified progress report he is to pass on to Nicky. It will not take long, once these papers are in the boss's hands and have been checked by enemy experts, for Peter to be revealed as a double agent. Things are speeding toward a climax.

Though Peter seems to be working with him and has given him the papers, Nicky is suspicious. "I'm watchin' you," he grumbles. "There's somepin wrong about your attitude." Lampier may trust Peter, but for the first time Nicky disagrees with his boss. "You give in too easy. You wasn't goin' to work with us one day, and the next day you was all ready to take orders . . . What I'm askin' myself is—why?"

The announcer lays out all the possibilities. "Time is what Peter is playing for . . . And time is running out . . . Nicky has time—all the time in the world . . . But for the FBI, desperately trying to unmask his boss, for the government agent following Nicky now—and for Peter himself—only days, perhaps hours, remain . . . For if Nicky once more is able to shake off surveillance—if he is able to reach his boss undetected—Peter will be revealed as a double agent, working for the government while he pretends to cooperate with the spy ring. The papers Nicky carries can easily prove to be his death warrant . . . You won't want to miss the exciting developments next week in the thrilling love story by Elaine Carrington—*Follow Your Heart*."

But there were to be no more exciting developments. After only three months, the program left the air.

With the clarity of hindsight, one might suggest that as the plot narrowed down to concentrate more and more on Peter's dangerous life as a counterspy, the program began to cross the boundary that divides soap opera from adventure serial, and thus lost its legitimate audience. It had started with a variety of promising soap themes, all of tried and proven interest. In fact, it should be admitted that this program began as a re-creation of the early days of one of radio's most successful shows, *When a Girl Marries*. The basic premise of wealthy socialite girl meets poor but promising boy, with its concomitant basic question (How can these two, coming from such different worlds, ever find happiness together?), echoes that of *WAGM*. And there are even closer correspondences. Julie's family situation agrees in detail with Joan Davis's. The long-separated but neighborly parents, the teen-aged sister, the engagement to the rich and suitable boy she does not really love, the gift of his family pearls.

Even the first meeting of the young lovers is the same: Harry Davis was mistaken for a piano tuner before Joan Field's engagement party back in 1937. Peter moves in with the friendly and intelligent, but essentially humble, MacKenzies. Harry in his day was befriended by Mrs. MacDonald, widow of a lawyer. Her daughter, Betty, had a fine legal mind and worked with Harry in her dead father's law library, which Mrs. MacDonald had invited him to use. Betty fell hopelessly in love with Harry, just as Georgie later would with Peter. In both cases, socialite mothers oppose their daughters' desire to break what they regard as suitable engagements in order to marry for love, and continually interfere in their daughters' lives. Both fathers, on the other hand, believe in love and encourage their daughters to pursue it at all costs.

When *Follow Your Heart* went off the air, *WAGM* was still on radio, where it would remain for six more years. Perhaps it was *FYH*'s efforts to move with the times, to grapple with what were felt to be more serious and adult themes, that proved its undoing. If it had concentrated more on the emotional struggles of its characters with each other, and less on rickety plotting based on world doom and public-spirited commitment to humanity, it might have developed and held a place for itself on television. It might even be with us still.

Two other programs introduced in 1951, *Search for Tomorrow* and *Love of Life,* confined themselves to private emotional conflict and managed to survive very nicely. *Search for Tomorrow* was the story of a widow, Joanne Tate, who has been played from the very beginning by the same actress, Mary Stuart. June 25, 1973, was the 5658th episode. Miss Stuart, talking about the character she portrays, has said, "I like the way she relates to people. She's very open and deeply interested in how others feel. This could also be a fault, of course, because often she cares too much and gets too involved."

TV Guide, describing *Search* in 1954, had this to say: "Frankly, tomorrow had better come soon for the characters on this show, before they all lose their minds . . . The people . . . keep searching for happiness . . . but they keep winding up in a hospital or a lawyer's office . . . The plot? Well, there's this widow who is in love with this man who either has a wife or hasn't, he isn't sure, and there is this other woman, in a hospital, who keeps saying she is so his wife. Whether she will ever walk again has not yet been disclosed. One thing, though—she can still see. Most times they go blind."

Love of Life began as the story of two sisters, Meg and Vanessa Dale. Vanessa, who loved life and thus provided the show's title, married but was soon widowed. Meg married and had a baby. By 1958 Meg was divorcing her husband. He had been blackmailing her new lover and was now accusing him of fathering her unborn child, though, as he well knew, the child was his own.

The sketchiest description is enough to identify the familiar terrain for us. This may be television we are hearing about, not radio, but assuredly we are back home in Soapland.

The Once and Future Soap

§

DAVID: You still can't say damn.

MADELEINE: No.

DAVID: Or h—

MADELEINE: Don't say it.

DAVID: Talk shows do it. Nighttime shows do it. Even birdies in the tr—

MADELEINE: I know, David-pal, but pull yourself together. Is that seriously your criterion for how serious the form is? How liberated? How real?

DAVID: Oh wow, heavy!

MADELEINE: Soaps practically lead the field in tackling social problems.

DAVID: Don't you ever get bored with being right?

MADELEINE: Not so far.

DAVID [*springing up*]: Oh, damn!

MADELEINE: Don't say it.

DAVID: Turn on the telly. We're missing our show! Maybe today she'll tell her husband that her unborn baby isn't his at all but was fathered by his drunken brother, a fact known to his political rival who is planning to blackmail him . . . [*But he is gone.*]

MADELEINE [*to camera, whimsically*]: Dear boy.

When the practitioners of today's soaps give interviews there's always a lot of talk about how the soaps have changed, how they've leaped into the forefront of topicality and relevance with their fearless, outspoken treatment of delicate and controversial themes. In olden days, they say, it was worth your working life to have a soap character sip anything more potent than a cup of cocoa. The hero of one radio soap told the heroine to say "ah" instead of "prunes" when he kissed her: the writer responsible for this breakthrough did not last long.

Indeed, the pruderies of bygone soaps are tiresomely well documented, and all the old stories are told and gleefully retold by those who want to demonstrate what a long, long way we have come since that dark age of innocence. Admirers of today's freedom delight in measuring the distance between now—when, as one producer explains, "the goodies can take a drink before dinner," though of course "without really slopping it up"—and the benighted time when Pepper Young, rashly permitted a bottle of beer on a hot day in the forties, called forth a spate of letters from indignant listeners.

No one would argue, of course, that soaps or their audiences are untouched by the currents of change. Recent soap opera has introduced such themes as impotence, abortion, drugs, incest, and miscegenation. Most of the children in Soapland are illegitimate; some of the people use language that might shock your great-aunt; strong drink is raging. But how much of a change does this represent? Were the good old days so sexless, conventional, and teetotal?

In the first place, the pruderies of radio soaps have been vastly exaggerated. Many of the "goodies" even during the most golden days of radio took social drinking for granted. In Elmwood or Springdale when the Robertses or the Hoyts arrived to have dinner with the Cotters or the Adamses, their in-laws, food was placed immediately before them. But when Vikki and Roger visited New York, drinks preceded dinner for everyone but Vikki, who was, after all, a very small-town nineteen. As for double beds, which have been claimed as a recent innovation of fearless TV soaps, many happy radio couples had them. Illegitimate children, to be sure, are relatively new to soap, but love affairs most certainly are not.

Television soaps have their arbitrary little pruderies too. Not long ago a famous TV soap writer used the word "virgin" in a script, only to have it removed by network censors. "Perhaps," she tartly remarked, "they don't believe there are any virgins any more."

Another TV soap suffered a prolonged dry spell because the producer decided that the leading characters, a school-teacher and his wife, who were frequently shown sharing a martini as they compared notes on their day's activities, were setting a bad example to the people out in Iowa. The social behavior of soap people, after all, has often reflected the personal standards of a writer living in New York or Hollywood, which do not much resemble Stanwood or Rosehill. In this case, the writer conceded that perhaps his characters were behaving atypically, considering their locale.

In the main, Soapland today is much as it was in radio days. The surface of life there has changed, just as the surface of American life in general has, but the basic, underlying assumptions that prevail there have not. Soaps are a long way from accepting, or even seeking, a new morality.

Alcoholism has always been a scourge in Soapland, and it still is, though alcoholics there are easier to rehabilitate than those in everyday life. Pat Randolph of *Another World* was a confirmed alcoholic for an even shorter period than Phil Stanley of radio's *When a Girl Marries.*

Drugs are never presented as a solution, but rather as a serious and disturbing problem, one that inevitably brings a terrible retribution. Infidelity exacts its price in guilt and self-contempt. The possibility of incest may titillate the viewer, but as soon as the principals (who naturally have no notion that they are brother and sister) realize the truth of their appalling situation they retreat precipitately from the unthinkable. The girl enters a convent.

Divorce, though sometimes necessary, is still a necessary evil. Soap characters do not easily divorce and then go on to find happiness with a new partner, though happiness may well be theirs after desertion by an unworthy spouse. The best way to end a marriage is still death.

Even Irna Phillips, the single most successful writer the soap world has ever known, must bow to this convention.

A few years ago on one of her shows a man left his wife for love of another woman. Miss Phillips' dashing plan was for the man to marry the other woman. His ex-wife would then fall in love with someone else. Everyone's romantic life would be, at least for a time, smooth.

But it was not to be: the network objected. "They told me I could go ahead and let the man divorce his wife," Miss Phillips explains, "but that I could not let his infidelity be rewarded by having him happily married to the other woman. It was either keep him around but miserable, or kill him off." Miss Phillips' solution was practical: "I killed him off. He went to Florida, fell over, and hit his head."

Soapland is still made up of small towns inhabited by professional men, chiefly doctors, and housewives. The towns, however small, contain whatever restaurants, gambling casinos, newspapers, hospitals, and factories may be required by the plot.

People still work mainly because they have to, and keep their careers in the dim background of their lives unless they happen to be doctors, in which case there is little division between career and private life. Doctors always interact with their patients on both a professional and a personal level.

Women, though some have a brief fling at a career, are even less likely to work than in radio days, though again doctors are an exception. A medical practice seems to combine well with domestic life, though some of these situations, given high marks by women's liberationists for showing women as professionally equal to men, have recently been under fire for failing to present the domestic side of egalitarianism in a realistic way. One woman doctor, whose office hours used to be arranged to suit the demands of motherhood (Dr. Maggie Powers began her professional day at eleven, returning home in time to see her daughter when she got out of school), is now allowed to work full time. But, as feminist critics point out, it is never explained how the housework of the professional women gets done, how the children are cared for, and what financial arrangements they make with their husbands.

Working women who pay attention to their careers are not

usually admirable. One woman doctor is shown neglecting her child in order to attend lectures at the hospital. One of the most successful businesswomen ever to appear on a television soap once helped embezzle huge sums from the company she worked for; her partner in crime suffered such pangs of guilt that he committed suicide, but the successful woman is made of stronger stuff. She is also extremely attractive to men, and thus belongs to that great class of unscrupulous soap women who prowl the business world, waiting to entice susceptible husbands.

This particular one has been murdered, but television soaps still have plenty of predatory females. Some of them do not work, but they all share the attributes of such radio soap temptresses as Claire O'Brien and Pamela Tower: they will lie, cheat, connive, in fact do anything necessary, to snatch the man they want away from his wife or fiancée. *Another World*'s Rachel Davis would have been right at home on radio, as would Lisa Hughes of *As the World Turns*.

Husbands are still hard to hang on to. Sometimes they are not entrapped by other women but simply disappear. Mrs. Dawson's Lewis of radio's *Rosemary* vanished no more inexplicably than Mrs. Foster's husband on today's *The Young and the Restless*. Mrs. Foster, like Mrs. Dawson in her day, resolutely opposes any suggestion that she have her husband declared legally dead and start looking for another man.

The soap heroine is usually a mature, experienced woman, as before, probably widowed at least once. As Dr. Jim, Mrs. Dawson's faithful suitor, once said, "Loving somebody's got nothing to do with the number of years you've spent on this earth. Susie, I couldn't love you more or want you more if I was twenty. Wouldn't know half as well at twenty how to take care of you and look after you as I do now—and maybe I wouldn't feel that there aren't too many years left for the happiness I want to bring you. Yes, loving somebody when you get to be our age is so darn much more important than when you're young."

Today's soap heroines may well have grown children with love affairs of their own, but such ladies as Joanne Tate and

Vanessa Sterling are still engaged in proving that, as Helen Trent always maintained, romance can exist at thirty-five and even beyond.

The heroine who starts out as a young, inexperienced girl is not given a long span of carefree youth. Sandy of *Bright Promise* begins her television life as a brilliant college student, but there is to be no protracted wandering in the groves of Academe for her. After an affair with one of her professors and a lengthy murder trial, she is plunged into the thickets of matrimony, complete with illegitimate child, jealous husband, and mysterious illness.

Despite their problems, the mature, experienced women of Soapland do their best to hold even the worst of marriages together; failing that, they try to provide good homes for their children. Whatever their marital status, they still spend a large part of their time in the kitchen. Servantless, they make pies, put up preserves, and serve popovers for ordinary family breakfasts. Their children rarely help.

Despite the family-centered domesticity of most of the characters, Soapland continues to be a violent place, where crime, disaster, and sudden death may disrupt the surface of life at any moment. Gangsters, drug dealers, members of the crime syndicate, may be plotting to take over the town, or to destroy the lives of the good characters by bending the weaker ones to their will. There are still many murders, for which an innocent person is usually tried. Lacking a tabulation, it cannot be proved that the number of killings and trials per soap-year has remained constant, but it seems a fairly safe guess. Television people still have not learned that when a person finds a dead body, his first action should not be to pick up the murder weapon.

On *The Guiding Light,* Peggy Dillman is charged with the murder of her husband Marty. During one of their frequent marital battles, Peggy was knocked unconscious and came to to find Marty dead. She herself thinks she may have killed him, but the murder turns out to have been committed by an unsavory character named Flip Malone.

On the same program, Stanley Norris is found shot in his

penthouse apartment. Among the suspects are his daughter Holly and a secretary who has been in love with him for years, but the prime suspect is his wife Leslie, who has discovered the body and left her fingerprints on the murder gun. This time, the amorous secretary's mother did it.

On *Another World,* Missy Palmer is married (supposedly in name only) to a con man named Danny Fargo. His old girl friend, Flo, stabs Danny in a fit of jealous rage. Missy, finding his body, picks up the knife and is tried for murder.

Walter Curtin, also a resident of Bay City, is involved in a shady deal with playboy Wayne Addison; Addison is murdered and Curtin's wife Lenore is seen leaving his apartment. She is tried and acquitted. Walter, the real criminal, is killed in an automobile accident before he can confess the truth.

On *As the World Turns* Lisa Hughes is married (but really in name only) to Dr. Michael Shea. He decides to prove her an unfit mother and take her young son away from her; she flees to Mexico with the child. That very night Shea is found dead. Lisa's older son, Tom, is tried for the crime and, believing his mother guilty, confesses. Fortunately, the real killer proves to be a woman with whom the unlamented Dr. Shea was having an affair.

Just as in radio days, the truth does come out, though it may take a long while. The innocent are vindicated; there is no miscarriage of justice. Good is still rewarded, albeit in grudging measure, and evil is punished—if not in the courts of men, at least in the higher court of accidental death.

There are still evil people in Soapland, though there is always some hope of eventual reform if they live long enough. One lasting villainess is Andrea Whiting, who not only broke up the engagement of her son Len and Patti Tate but has attempted, during her long tenure on *Search for Tomorrow,* to kill a number of people. She was responsible, years ago, for the death of Len's twin, and tried to blame it on her husband.

Back in the fifties, on radio's *When a Girl Marries,* a vindictive alcoholic developed such a passionate jealousy of Harry Davis that he contrived his own suicide to look like murder, carefully arranging clues to ensure that suspicion would fall on Harry.

In the seventies the same thing happens on a television soap, *The Doctors,* when Dr. Allison, in a paroxysm of resentment, kills himself in order to make everyone think Dr. Aldrich has murdered him. Perhaps today's soap writers unconsciously learned their craft by listening to radio, and then again perhaps the fact that both of these maleficent suicides are named Allison is the purest (ninety-nine and forty-four one hundredths per cent pure) coincidence.

The presence of so many evil people in Soapland does, as ever, provide opportunity for adventure. Heroines who might otherwise remain peacefully in kitchen or hospital are frequently forced into dangerous action by the wicked. Radio's Rosemary Dawson, searching for her husband's child, innocently provokes a desperate character. She is immediately abducted and sequestered in an isolated cabin, where she is left in the dark to fear rats, rape, and eventual death by starvation. Only her quick-wittedness in managing to leave a note behind enables the police to find her. On television's *Somerset,* Andrea is lured to an isolated cabin by her jealous stepsister, who fully intends to shoot her. The arrival of another sibling by last-minute helicopter saves Andrea as dramatically as Stella Dallas ever rescued her daughter Laurel.

Much of the excitement in the life of the soap heroine is provided by physiological or psychosomatic disaster. Indeed it would be the labor of a lifetime to tabulate all the diseases to which soap flesh has been subject. The most interesting and useful, and therefore frequently recurring, impairments are those that leave the character still able to participate in the action. He can lie immobilized in an oxygen tent or anesthetized under the surgeon's knife for only a brief period before the audience's interest is perforce transferred to other characters. Suspense can, of course, center on whether or not the character will die, but more fruitful to the plot is a chronic condition. Then two questions arise: first, Will it be permanent? and second, If it does prove lasting, how will it affect the future course of the character's life? Thus paralysis, blindness, and amnesia are the afflictions of choice.

Men in Soapland are still frequently relegated for longer

or shorter periods to the wheelchair; though television soap wives are perhaps a little likelier to become emotionally involved elsewhere than their radio counterparts were, they do remain faithful. Blindness, too, continues unabated. Joanne Tate of *Search for Tomorrow* has lost her vision for both physical and psychological reasons, though no television heroine's sightlessness has yet rivaled the complex etiology of Ellen Brown's, which resulted from an allergy, particularly unfortunate in the proprietress of a tearoom, to chocolate cake.

Amnesia has been a soap staple almost from the outset. Some researchers credit Jane Cruisinberry, creator of *The Story of Mary Marlin,* with its introduction. Back in the thirties she inflicted what they claim was radio's first case on Joe Marlin, Mary's husband. His amnesia proved intractable, and he spent years wandering through Asia, known only as Mr. X. The restoration of his memory heralded the doom of the program, since his return to the United States precipitated Mary's political decline, she having been Joe's replacement in the Senate. When Mary regained a husband, she lost her job, her presidential beau, and her audience.

Irna Phillips has also been credited with introducing amnesia into Soapland, and, while she is willing to accept the accolade, she is careful to distinguish two classes of affliction. "My amnesia," she insists, "was induced by a blow on the head." Deploring its frequent use in other people's soaps, she condescendingly points out that "after a while it got so the only way people on serials got amnesia was through a psychological shock. There's a difference."

A difference there may be, but there's also a sameness. During an amnesic spell, all kinds of changes can take place in a character or a situation, changes that could never otherwise be achieved. It seems safe to predict that so useful a device will not lightly be surrendered by soap writers.

In recent years many characters have been afflicted with one type or the other. Lisa Hughes, when she appears in court just in time to hear her son confess to the murder of her husband, collapses. Returning consciousness fails to bring memory in its wake, and for a long time she suspects that she may be a murderess. Phillip Brent of *All My Children* discovers the facts about his illegitimate parentage, loses his memory, and leaves for New York, completely forgetting his love for his longtime sweetheart, Tara Martin. And on *Days of Our Lives* an amnesic veteran of the Korean War returns, unrecognizably transformed by plastic surgery. Since he and his family neither recognize nor remember each other, he falls in love with his own sister.

Another plot device as useful now as it ever was in radio days is the social gap. Just as two lovers almost inevitably came from two different worlds in radio soaps, so do they still on television. Democracy has by no means made the people of Soapland equal, and they are conscious of many kinds of social barriers. She may be a daughter of the town's leading family and he the son of the local garage mechanic, cleaning woman, or factory worker. Or her father may run the local casino, which makes her an unsuitable match for a young lawyer or doctor. She can be an orphan of unknown parentage; he can be illegitimate.

Sometimes the gap is not strictly a social one, but depends upon what might be called the principle of the impossible love object. The characters yearn for each other, but circumstances put their love out of the question. He is a priest; she is pregnant by someone else; he belongs to the wrong ethnic group; she is his brother's wife, or even his own sister.

The principle of the impossible love object has its associated and almost inevitable activity: going out of somebody's life forever. This is done by impossible love objects to save their lovers pain; they know that their continued presence can only bring unhappiness to anyone who cares for them. Indeed, going out of someone's life forever is a noble and virtuous action. Fortunately, this step can be taken without permanently ending the relationship. The impossible love object usually returns, or is tracked down, and proves not to be impossible after all.

A prototypical radio case is that of Bill Roberts, who is an impossible love object because he suffers from amnesia and thus cannot know what dark things may suddenly return from his unknown past to inflict suffering on Rosemary, the girl he loves. He consults her mother about his decision to go out of her life forever.

BILL: What right have I got to tie up her life like that? . . . What right have I got to make such a demand on her loyalty and her love? I haven't, Mrs. Dawson, and I won't . . . I think—I think I ought to go away from here for a while—don't you think so? Tell me honestly, don't you think so?

MOTHER: Oh, Bill, this is the hardest decision I've ever had to make in my life—

BILL: I'm not going to count *me* any more—I'm not important in this. Until I do know who I am, I've got to go away . . . I've got to leave here and—and give her a chance to forget me. But I love her so much, Mrs. Dawson, that I'm not going to stop to count the cost to myself—I'm not going to stop and think about myself . . . I don't matter in this thing at all . . . I'm just somebody that the tide washed in to your shore—somebody who was almost drowned, and you and Rosemary and Patti brought back to life again. And now—now let the tide wash me out again.

MOTHER: Oh, Bill . . . I wish with all my heart and soul that it wasn't the right thing for you to do this—

BILL: But it is, isn't it, Mrs. Dawson?

MOTHER [*with difficulty*]: Yes, Bill—it is.

Soap people still see this as the right, indeed the only, thing to do in certain circumstances. On *Another World,* Missy Palmer, an orphan ignorant of her parentage, discovers on the eve of her wedding that she is illegitimate. Now an impossible love object, and truly loving her fiancé, Bill Matthews, she decides to go out of his life forever. By the time Bill finds her again, she has married another man, but eventually they do find a brief happiness together.

Lee Randolph, another girl on the program, is not so fortunate. She has inadvertently taken LSD, which was slipped into her coffee by a hoodlum called Lefty. From that time on, fearing chromosome damage, she too is an impossible love object. Accordingly, she goes out of the life of Sam Lucas, the man she loves. Since Lee is killed during one of her LSD-induced recurring hallucinations, she is one of the very few to succeed in making forever really mean forever.

Parenthood is still of great importance in Soapland. There are still mothers who find the entire meaning of their lives in their children. Mrs. Holden, mother of ex-mental patient and suspected child molester Philip Holden of *Love of Life,* has no life at all aside from her boy. Not only is he an only child and she a widow, but she has not another relative or friend in the whole wide world. When Philip is depressed, of course, it is not enough to offer him a cup of coffee, as Mrs. Davis would have done to Harry; his problems are too alarming for that. But Mrs. Holden does her best to comfort him when the story of his past begins to circulate in Rosehill.

MRS. HOLDEN: You expect so much of people. You always have.

PHILIP: Well, go ahead and say it, Mother.

MRS. HOLDEN: Say what?

PHILIP: That you told me so. That you always said if anyone ever knew this story—it'd be the end of me here in Rosehill. You warned me and I wouldn't believe you—and you turned out to be right.

MRS. HOLDEN: Son, I didn't want to be right about this. I just wish I could have spared you the pain of finding it out this way.

PHILIP: Well, now the question is—what do I do?

MRS. HOLDEN: If you decided to leave town, I'd understand. And I'd be ready to leave anytime you want.

PHILIP: But you don't want to leave. You've got the kind of life you want here.

MRS. HOLDEN: Wherever you go, that's where I want to be.

PHILIP: You've made so many sacrifices for me. Too bad they've all been wasted.

MRS. HOLDEN: Now, Philip—I know that someday you're going to be someone very outstanding—and I'm going to be proud of you. I'm proud of you now.

PHILIP: Your son who's had such a successful career? Murder suspect, ex-mental patient? What a wonderful record.

MRS. HOLDEN: You're a very gifted boy. Everybody knows that.

PHILIP: Sure, gifted at starting things I don't finish, gifted at thinking but not doing. And now . . . now I'm making it impossible for you to live where you want.

MRS. HOLDEN: Philip, don't you know you're the most important thing in the world to me—and there's nothing I wouldn't do if I thought it was for your good?

PHILIP: Yes, I do know that, Mother. But it doesn't make much of a life for you, does it?

MRS. HOLDEN [*her arms around him*]: Oh, Philip—who ever said life was going to be easy . . . for any of us?

Even the most questionable women in Soapland, like Lisa Hughes, are concerned about their children. Lisa once broke off with a millionaire who was courting her, because he discouraged his daughter's relationship with her son Tom. Some mothers, as always, are too deeply concerned, and meddle in their children's romantic lives. This is still a self-defeating mistake.

The maternal impulse stands firmly in the way of abortion. A Soapland woman need not possess an admirable character to reject a surgical solution to her problems, however acceptable it may have become in the real world. Barbara Sterling of *Love of Life,* a self-centered, spoiled, mentally unstable girl who found herself divorced and pregnant, and whose life would obviously be immensely complicated by the addition of a child, is forced to abandon the idea of abortion. At the bus station, on her way to the abortionist, Barbara minds a stranger's baby while she makes a phone call. The helpless little creature melts Barbara's heart and she decides to bear her child after all. Susie, of *Days of Our Lives,* changes her mind about abortion at the very last moment, after actually checking in at the hospital.

Most Soapland women still consider having a baby one of their chief goals in life. They may not always reach the euphoric peaks described by Mrs. Dawson when she told her daughter, "I don't think anything's so wonderful as having children. I don't think anyone's so lucky as a mother." Sometimes they are frankly unhappy about the prospect of imminent motherhood. But since everyone else so heartily approves of their condition, they are eventually won over.

On *Days of Our Lives* a forty-five-year-old woman becomes pregnant, to everyone's delight. On *The Doctors*, Althea tells Carolee, "I'm so envious of you—you and your beautiful baby." *Love of Life*'s Kate, unsure that she wants to bear a child, is advised, "Don't let any feelings of uncertainty keep you from having a baby." And Diana, unhappily pregnant on *General Hospital*, is encouraged as enthusiastically as Mrs. Dawson herself might have done it: "Motherhood is the most wonderful experience a woman can have. Think of the first time the baby splashes you in the bathtub, the first time he sleeps through the night without crying."

The actual birth rate on television soaps exceeds that of radio. Within one year babies were born to Janet on *Search for Tomorrow*, Meredith on *One Life to Live*, Edie on *All My Children*, Angel on *Love Is a Many Splendored Thing*, Diana on *General Hospital*, Linda on *Days of Our Lives*, Mary on *Where the Heart Is*, and Carolee of *The Doctors*. *Another World*'s Pat Randolph, her sterility cured by an operation, gave birth to twins.

During that same year a number of other TV ladies became pregnant: both Kate and Mrs. Donovan on *Love of Life*, Kathy on *The Doctors*, India on *Somerset*, Jane on *General Hospital*, Iris on *Love Is a Many Splendored Thing*, and Tara on *All My Children*.

A great majority of TV's pregnancies are accidental. Sometimes they result from one night of unpremeditated or unwilling passion, but sometimes, surprisingly, the presumably well-educated, middle-class participants in a continuing affair seem never to have heard of birth control.

The soap audience can only assume that the impulse to procreate is so strong it cannot be denied. The unmistakable message is that man and woman are bound together almost against their will by an overriding impulse toward parenthood. To resist this natural result would be somehow to fall short of full humanity. A love that does not aim itself powerfully toward childbearing is incomplete, hollow, and cannot last.

Acknowledging the truth of this, television women continually try to win men to them by pregnancy. Despite everything experience and common sense might suggest, the TV woman believes that bearing his child will keep her man from straying. Susan, on *As the World Turns,* senses that her husband, Dan, is attracted to another woman. In this she is correct: he is not only in love with someone else but has proved it by fathering her child. Susan, attempting to hold Dan, manages to become pregnant.

Another unhappy wife, Allison on *Where the Heart Is,* does her utmost to seduce her estranged husband so that she can become pregnant like Chris, the woman he loves. He rejects her advances: his loyalty is to Chris, mother of his unborn child.

Women often do succeed in binding a man to them through pregnancy. That failing, they may later win him over through the resulting child. Many a man in Soapland enjoys visiting a baby he has inadvertently fathered, thereby involving himself more deeply with the mother. On *Another World,* for example, Rachel seduces Stephen Frame. That does not work, but through their baby Stephen is eventually captured.

Since the ability to bear children is so important, the lack of it is considered tragic. Many of Soapland's women carry about with them the gnawing pain of knowing that they are incomplete, women who can never be mothers. This has been a problem with Vanessa on *Love of Life,* Pat of *Another World* (though in her case it turns out to be operable), and many others. Women who miscarry are as deeply upset by it as radio women were in similar circumstances. Nowadays they are likely to seek psychiatric help. A hysterectomy has a yet greater impact. Sandy, heroine of *Bright Promise,* though she already has a baby, is in despair at the prospect. "Empty, empty, empty," she cries hysterically. "I'll never feel life inside me again!"

Men, too, suffer deeply if incapable of fatherhood. Nick Davis of *All My Children* has marital problems; he invests his wife Ann's money unwisely in a friend's business, and the friend absconds with it. But the decisive factor in the breakup of the marriage is Nick's belief that he is unable to father a child.

Mickey on *Days of Our Lives* is aware that his wife has had an affair with his brother, but he cannot be told that her child is the result of that affair. If he knew that, the fact of his own sterility might emerge; the dreadful knowledge of this inadequacy would, his wife, father, and brother all agree, destroy him.

On *General Hospital* a man who has been made impotent in an accident is more upset by the loss of his ability to father a child than by mere sexual inability. Looking back on better days, he muses longingly: "Diana—feeding *my son.* I'll never forget it. It was beautiful, just beautiful. That must be what it's all about. My God! How I've been robbed!"

The most important subject of everyone's interest, however, the summit of everyone's desire, the apex of hope, is still love. Above all, married love.

Since everyone's ambition is to be happily married, how is it to be managed? Soaps are still turning this question around endlessly. We are shown a variety of marriages in the process of being arranged, enjoyed, endured, or disintegrated. We are made fully aware of just what has been invested in the relationship on both sides. Then, by assessing the happiness of the participants, we can judge for ourselves whether a marriage so constituted can, or should, long endure.

In radio's *When a Girl Marries,* Phil Stanley proposes to Eve Topping out of jealous bravado, to show Joan Davis, who has left him for another man, that he can live without her. Eve accepts him, knowing exactly what the situation is. "I just happen to be head over heels in love with you," she tells him. "You're not in love with me—that's just my hard luck. But I think I can love enough for both of us."

They elope, and the announcer considers the questions raised by a one-sided relationship. "And so," he says, "for better or for worse, Phil and Eve are married. We know that, for the moment at least, Eve is very happy—for she was willing to have Phil whether he loved her or not. But we wonder if Phil was playing fair with Eve in taking this final step, when deep down inside he's still in love with someone else. Is Eve right in thinking she can make Phil forget his feeling for Joan? Will her marriage be worth the price, as she seems to think?"

In *Love of Life* there is a very similar problem, though this time it is the man who undertakes to love enough for both. Barbara, who is not in love with Tony, discusses the problem with her grandmother, and they try to decide what kind of relationship is necessary for happiness in marriage.

BARBARA: I honestly believe it is right for me to marry Tony.

VIVIAN: Then what's worrying you, Barbara? For an engaged girl you're certainly not looking at all happy.

BARBARA: I know. [*sighs.*] I don't know what's the matter with me. I know I ought to be feeling happier than I do . . . but I just don't, Grandma. You do want me to tell you the truth, don't you?

VIVIAN: Barbara, dear, Tony's going to be a very successful man one day, I'm sure of it. And you're going to live the kind of life you want—the kind of life you should have been living all along.

BARBARA: It sounds right, Grandma . . . it sounds like just what I want. But if I don't feel it . . . maybe it's not what I want, really. Do you know what I'm talking about?

VIVIAN: It sounds like a bad case of nerves, that's all.

BARBARA: But you see . . . if I really loved Tony, I'd be happier, wouldn't I? I know I depend on him . . . I need him . . . but I don't know if I love him enough.

VIVIAN: Oh, love! Barbara, you're not sixteen years old any more. The kind of love you need to build a good marriage is not the kind of love you see in the movies, or the kind of thing they sing about . . . you'll make yourself very unhappy if you try to base a marriage on that kind of romantic infatuation.

BARBARA: Do you think it's right to marry someone you're not in love with, Grandma?

VIVIAN: You say you depend on Tony—you need him. You trust each other, and you want the same kind of life. Well, that's love—the kind of love to base a marriage on. Those are the things that last . . . things that are real, not the result of some temporary illusion.

BARBARA: Oh, Grandma, nothing is as simple as I thought it was going to be . . .

VIVIAN: You know what I think, Barbara? Once you and Tony are married, all these doubts and hesitations will disappear once and for all.

BARBARA: I hope you're right.

VIVIAN: And I'll tell you something else. You shouldn't wait. You and Tony should get married immediately. Barbara, I'm sure I'm right about this.

Barbara's grandmother upholds the view of love and marriage that Mrs. Field used to express to her daughter Joan in radio days, when she urged her to marry the suitable Phil Stanley instead of the object of her girlish fancy, Harry Davis. This is the same outlook espoused by Mrs. Fielding in early television days when she argued the issue with her daughter Julie. It is the sane and sensible view rejected by most soap heroines; those who accept it in haste are sure to repent it at leisure.

This time the other side of the controversy is taken by Tony's mother, who believes that marriage must be based on intense romantic feeling. Barbara, trying to make friends with her future mother-in-law, tells Mrs. Vento that she believes the two of them can settle their past differences. After all, she says, "Both of us are people who . . ." She hesitates, unable to finish her sentence without using the word "love," which she cannot quite bring herself to do, and concludes, "who . . . who are very fond of Tony." Immediately grasping the implications of this, Mrs. Vento is stricken. "Fond?" she cries. "You do feel more than that for Tony, don't you?" Barbara still cannot respond, and Mrs. Vento continues: "Because if you don't have any more feeling for him than that . . . oh, please, tell him now. Don't hurt him again! It would be the cruelest thing in the world to marry him if you don't love him. Please!" Then she bursts into tears.

As things turn out, Barbara's marriage to Tony is even more disastrous than Eve's to Phil. Total emotional commitment is once again demonstrated to be the necessary foundation of marriage.

The one area where television soaps unquestionably differ from the radio variety is that of sexual explicitness. But whether their erotic impact has thereby been increased is certainly debatable. Considering the nature of audience identification, it may in fact have been diminished.

Today's liberated soaps offer examples of actual rape. On

Somerset, while Ginger's husband is out of town, an unscrupulous business associate rapes her and departs with the threat that if she tells her husband he will swear that she cooperated eagerly. They both know the husband will believe it. This kind of rape, a helpless woman forced into submission and unable to hope for any kind of victory, even a moral one, hardly invites audience identification. Imaginative participation in indignity and failure is not pleasant.

Radio offered no such dismal and disheartening spectacle; quite the opposite. For one thing, the would-be radio rapist is possessed by violent and uncontrollable passion. His may be a twisted mind, to be sure, but he has chosen his woman like any other romantic lover. Radio soap heroines were innocent and tended to forget just how irresistible they were to the twisted minds among the menfolk. But the listener was quite aware of the impact the charms of a woman like Mary Noble might be expected to exert, and recognized the first signs of incipient abduction long before the heroine guessed that anything was amiss. Again and again, on soap after soap, love-crazed villains (often foreign) enticed or kidnaped beautiful ladies to remote cabins, towers, harems, and hunting lodges, there alternately to threaten and woo them until they were—and they always were—somehow saved in the nick of time.

The listener had the comfortable security of knowing that nothing truly dreadful would be allowed to happen to the heroine, so she could thoroughly enjoy considering all the dread possibilities inherent in the situation. Of course, when someone else must come to the rescue of the heroine, whether it be Stella Dallas saving her daughter from the sheik's harem or faithful suitor Gil Whitney wresting Helen Trent from the clutches of a mad German, the woman is still seen as rather a helpless creature, to be endangered or saved, in trouble or in triumph, only by the grace of other people. A more satisfying deliverance to contemplate is that effected by the heroine herself, when her own resourcefulness extricates her from danger. This way the audience has the best of both worlds: it can agonize with the captive and threatened heroine, feverishly plot and plan her escape, and then share her exultant self-sufficiency when she is able to reach safety.

Joan Field Davis of *When a Girl Marries* was abducted in a particularly exciting manner in the fifties. The twisted mind in this case belongs to a man known as Dr. Donald Brady. The audience knows that though he truly is a doctor, he has assumed the identity of the real Donald Brady, who died under mysterious circumstances and bore an uncanny resemblance to our mad villain. They also know that he is being blackmailed because he has practiced euthanasia on his own child and possibly murdered his wife as well. This embittered criminal, then, is called to the bedside of Joan Davis's youngest child, who has contracted pneumonia. Throughout the night, Joan bravely remains at the bedside of the stricken child, comporting herself with such impressive maternal devotion that the man known as Donald Brady falls in love with her. He correctly senses that Joan and her husband have had some kind of misunderstanding; he knows that she plans a visit to her sister in France. A few days later he suggests to her that he, too, may be in France soon to settle some family business, and asks if he may see her there.

When she arrives in France and arranges to rent a little house next door to her sister's, she discovers Donald Brady already in residence in the apartment over the garage. It sounds like a convenient arrangement, and one conducive to seduction; no doubt the audience was by this time agreeably suspicious. But a situation like this was pedestrian, compared with the heights of exoticism that would eventually be scaled. A new web of deception and complication was to open up for Joan Davis in the next few weeks.

First it turns out that the owner of the house Joan is renting (and the garage in which Donald is elaborating his febrile schemes) is married to Joan's old boarding-school roommate. They spend most of their time in Nice, which is why they are willing to rent their Parisian pied-à-terre. What then could be more natural than for Joan to wish to visit her old friend—and to accept a ride with Donald Brady, who happens to be heading in that direction on business. After all, he did save her baby.

Then the audience is let into another level of Donald Brady's secret life. Apparently he has a hold on a woman named Rosa who owns a chateau in the south of France. He has arranged with her that Joan is to be brought there and held prisoner. If Rosa does not cooperate, he will reveal her shameful past as a collaborationist during the war.

On the trip south Donald drugs Joan's fruit juice. When they reach the bend in the road next to the chateau, Rosa and a helper appear, to spirit the unconscious Joan away. Donald —as ever, fearlessly criminal—drives the car over the guard-rail, managing to leap clear just before it plunges over a cliff into the Mediterranean.

When Joan regains consciousness she is lying, exquisitely robed, in a huge canopy bed amid priceless antiques in the most beautiful room she has ever seen. Her blond hair has been dyed black, her fair complexion artfully stained brown. Donald explains that he and she are now both dead as far as the world will ever know; now they can begin a new and perfect life together. All she has to do is forget husband and children and learn to love him as he so desperately does her.

This fantasy world in which a woman is held captive firmly yet adoringly, with every kindness and luxury supplied, must have been an enjoyable one for the audience mind to dwell in; and dwell it could over a period of months, as the frantic search for Joan continued, the proof of her death was accepted, and the mourning for her begun. There was absolutely no escape for the poor girl, since the approaches to the chateau were trapdoored and mined; and if she did somehow get out she would immediately be returned by anyone who found her, since the story had been carefully established that she was Rosa's daughter, crazed and deluded into thinking that the spirit of the dead American had entered her body.

In the end, as the audience had all along known she eventually would, Joan (an invincible woman) did manage to escape. Returning to the United States, she had to face the fact that her husband, believing her dead, had married another woman—but that, of course, is another plot sequence.

Joan's incarceration in the luxurious tower offers the audience several very attractive prospects. In the first place, it is pleasant to dwell on the fact that men may be crazed by the desirability of women. And the charm that lures a man is not necessarily superficial: one need not be in the first flush of youth, or coruscatingly witty, or brilliant and successful. It helps, of course, to be lovely, but real loveliness seems to reside in some quality of womanliness, as demonstrated by Joan's loving all-night vigil beside Junior's crib. Even the twisted mind sees how beautiful and hopeful life might be with the right woman—who is, it appears, an average housewife.

Then there is the immense attention Donald must pay to obtaining his objective. How he must desire Joan, to devise so elaborate a courtship, dependent as it is on dyes and drugs, blackmail and extortion, and placing as it does such demands on his resources, mental, physical, and financial. And Donald, despite his twisted mind, is a pretty dashing fellow. Taking into account all his past crimes, discussed and implied, he has had a remarkably varied and exciting life. Handsome as he is, and, we must assume, irresistible to women (even the put-upon Rosa murmurs that Joan is lucky to have won the love of such a man), he has paid no attention to romance since some ambiguous betrayal suffered at the hands of that long-ago wife. He has not, then, really loved before. Being the only woman an attractive criminal has ever truly loved has a certain cachet.

Identifying with a heroine in such a situation as Joan's, the listener can consider all kinds of exciting possibilities, enjoy participating in them vicariously without accepting any responsibility for them—after all, she didn't think them up, did she?—and then virtuously reject them.

This kind of imaginative participation in other lives is the chief satisfaction the soaps have always offered their audiences. The process of vicarious acceptance, satiation, and eventual rejection leads to a renewed acceptance of the audience's own life, a reconciliation that, if any other form but soap opera were under discussion, might be called catharsis.

Soap Watchers

§

MADELEINE: Just look at all the letters coming in. You see, they haven't forgotten.

DAVID: I think we should disregard the bomb threats and the mash notes. Just concentrate on the loving personal notes from ardent fans. And I don't think we should tell them that we are real people. They seem perfectly content to keep their fantasies.

MADELEINE: Here's a sweet one. From a lady in Ocala. "Keep up the good work. I love my stories and I'm wearing my Helen Trent for President button to Bohack's every day. Where do you buy your darling earrings? And tell David I like him better with his hair short. He doesn't look as creepy."

DAVID: Go on.

MADELEINE: "Tell Rick that the baby is not his and Barbara should get lost. I just think she is a bitch. How did she ever get on television?"

DAVID: A bit strong, methinks.

MADELEINE: I think it's very healthy. Gives the audience a chance to vent their pent-up hostilities, affords them a full emotional life that they may lack at home. I think it's . . . very touching.

DAVID: Here, use my handkerchief.

MADELEINE: Let's see what some of the other letters say . . .

Who are you, anyway? Well, of course, you are you, and you may resent being categorized, but the networks like to think they know who you are and they spend a lot of money finding out.

It's a safe bet that you belong to a household that has a television set. In 1972, 96 per cent of all American households did. And most of those (53 per cent) were color sets. If you don't have a color set yet, you'd better catch up or you won't fit into the network's idea of who you are.

Thirty per cent of all television households watch daytime television. In 1972, the average number of homes viewing daytime TV was 18.6 million.

Are you one of them? Does it give you a sense of belonging?

Chances are four to one that you are a woman, since fewer than 20 per cent of daytime viewers are men.

Seventy-six per cent of nonworking women watch TV in the daytime.

You say you are a working woman? You still can't get out of it so easily, since 54 per cent of you still find time to view TV in the daytime. That makes a nifty statistic: 65 per cent of all women watch daytime television. This percentage has remained quite constant since 1968.

If you are an average woman (are you willing to own up to that?) you watch your telly from Monday through Friday between 10 A.M. and 5 P.M. for an average of over seven hours each week. And if the trend continues, you will watch even more.

And, although game and quiz shows grab a slight lead among older women (those fifty and over), younger women, you may be glad to know (those eighteen to fifty), prefer the indomitable soap opera.

Afternoon shows draw larger audiences than those before 1 P.M., especially among you "younger" women. More of you "older" women form a majority of the morning watchers.

Although the variance is slight, more of you watch on Fridays and Mondays, tapering off in your loyalty only mildly on Tuesday, Wednesday, and Thursday.

You have your favorites, of course, but even those you watch an average of only a little over three times a week. But you are loyal. And you tend to watch your stories in blocks of an hour or an hour and a half. You set for yourself a very strong viewing pattern, carefully established to conform with whatever else may demand your time and attention.

You tend to watch a little more in the fall, then a little less during the winter, and by summer you are watching less than you've watched all year.

See! They know all about you!

It is quite possible that you are a soap watcher, perhaps even a fan, and do not fit into this computerized idea of the typical viewer, into the democratic majority that the surveys say makes up the daytime serial audience. You may be surprised to discover (perhaps for the first time in your life) that you belong to a largely ignored, often underprivileged minority group. This may cause you a bit of pride or be the cause of some anxiety, but there is no help for it. The surveys have been made, the ratings rated.

If you have managed to keep within the Average Viewer Club you will be happy to know that what you see on your daytime television screen is meant for you, the vast soap opera audience and potential consumer.

It is you, the audience, who determine what shows stay on the air year after year, which are short-lived, and, indeed, which new ones are born on the airwaves. You determine the ratings.

You read and hear a lot about the ratings. You are told that such-and-such is going off because it is low in the ratings. Or that this other one is constantly high in the ratings. The first may be your favorite; the other you may not like at all. But *c'est,* as they say, *la vie.*

One of the earliest ways to determine the popularity of a radio soap was to tabulate the response to premium offers made on the air to the listeners. Flower seeds, cheap earrings, and the like—all heavily endorsed by the leading character of the serial—were offered on the air to the public.

Some minimal charge, usually ten cents, was made, and the listener also sent in a boxtop or wrapper from the product as proof of purchase. Responses were usually in the tens of thousands, satisfying the producer's curiosity, proving not only that there were people listening but that they were buying the product as well.

The "offer" was often made after weeks of buildup. A character in the show would mention the heroine's lovely earrings. They would be spoken of again and again as a not-so-integral part of the story—or perhaps even worked into the plot. The discerning listener learned to suspect that eventually an offer would be made. She, too, could have a lavaliere designed by Mary Noble or a Love Bird Pin just like Helen Trent's, with "real simulated-gold flashing." Ma Perkins' flower seeds were in great demand, as was a can opener said to have been invented by Lorenzo Jones.

The earliest research company in the field was founded by Archibald Crossley in 1930 and was called the Cooperative Analysis of Broadcasting. It issued what were called the CAB, or Crossley, ratings. Many people predicted that this kind of audience assessment would improve broadcasting.

Today, although there are a number of research companies that are used for special rating services (Trendex and Hooper, for instance), it is Nielsen that dominates the ratings field.

The A. C. Nielsen Company is a large research firm that gathers most of its revenue from doing market research on food and drug products for advertisers and their agencies. Almost as a sideline, in terms of revenue, Nielsen also conducts the audience-measurement research that is paid for by the networks, advertising agencies, and advertisers.

The audience data they pay for come in two primary forms: the rating and the share.

The rating is a figure that indicates the percentage of all existing TV homes (of which there are approximately 66 million these days) actually tuned to a particular program at a given moment. Most soaps have a rating around 7.0 or 8.0. That means that 7 per cent (or 8 per cent) of the homes equipped with television were tuned to that program at the time the survey specifies. Seven per cent may not sound great to you, but that percentage of households includes about 7 million people. Seven per cent is good.

The share of audience is a figure indicating the percentage

of all homes actually using TV that are tuned to a particular program. A share of thirty (30 per cent of the audience) does not seem at first glance to be particularly impressive, since there are only three major networks and you might think it would be easy to collect a third of the viewers. But because of independent stations and educational stations, each of which claims some small share, a share of thirty is very good indeed.

There are many methods of obtaining the data used to compute the ratings: telephone calls, door-to-door personal interviews, diaries that the viewers keep, and electronic monitoring devices attached to television sets to record the times they were used and which channels were watched.

The Nielsen ratings are gleaned from the viewing information provided by 3400 television homes. Two methods are used: the diary and the Audimeter.

The Audimeter, an electronic recording device, is placed in 1200 homes to monitor the tuning activity of all sets in the household. The sample families are given a few dollars a month and reimbursed for one half of all their TV repair bills. The meter, which does not require attention by the family, is equally accurate at all times of the day. Connected by phone line to Nielsen's computers, the meters automatically turn in their tuning records at least twice a day. These records, of course, tell only which programs were viewed.

To find out who actually did the viewing, a different method is employed. In a separate sample, 2200 homes keep diaries indicating who in the family, by age and sex, was watching what—providing what Nielsen refers to as "persons-viewing information." Since diary families would soon quit if requested to keep up their diaries week after week, only a third of them record their viewing during any given week. The diary homes are active only thirty weeks out of the year, so each family keeps a record during ten weeks a year. The rule is that there must be a turnover of 20 per cent yearly in the Audimeter home sample and 30 per cent in the diary sample so that no family can serve more than five years. This is meant to prevent .005 per cent of the country's population from continually dictating the public taste.

The information relayed by the Audimeter is combined with

that gathered in the diaries, collated—and behold, the ratings are made.

It is difficult to understand how these 1200 Audimeter-equipped homes and 2200 diary homes, together representing only 3400 TV families, can accurately reflect the viewing habits of total America, potentially almost 200 million viewers. Nielsen claims that the data-forwarding families represent a true cross section of all viewers in regard to educational levels, income brackets, and sex and age categories. But it may be noted that the illiterate are, of necessity, excluded from diary samples (though not from the meter sample). It is also hard to imagine a Park Avenue matron sending the butler out to mail the weekly diary to Nielsen in Chicago, even with the incentive of a dollar or so. But the fact remains that the networks regard the ratings as gospel, and studies of the system show that the information collected does reflect quite accurately the viewing habits of the country.

These various ratings, then, indicate how many viewers are watching, and sometimes also their sex, age, economic status, and educational level. They do not, however, in any way reflect the viewers' taste or the viewers' opinion of what they see. It is assumed that if the ratings of a show remain high, it is a show that the public wants. Whether the show is valuable, constructive, healthy, entertaining, or any good whatsoever is another story.

In the 1972–73 season there were fifteen soaps on the air, and this is the way they stood in the Nielsen ratings:

As the World Turns	10.6
Days of Our Lives	9.9
Another World	9.8
General Hospital	9.6
The Doctors	9.2
Search for Tomorrow	8.5
The Guiding Light	8.3
One Life to Live	8.1
All My Children	8.1
The Edge of Night	8.0

Return to Peyton Place	7.2
Love of Life	6.9
Somerset	6.8
The Secret Storm	6.5
The Young and the Restless	5.2

A great deal of money has been invested in finding out who watches soaps, and much more to determine how many watch. Some has even been spent to determine just why people watch soap opera at all and exactly what the soaps' perpetual appeal may be.

Over the years, psychologists and sociologists have come up with various ideas. Like all generalizations, they are presumptuous, some seem specious, many are inconclusive. Yet there is some parcel of truth in these assumptions, if taken with a grain of soap.

Soap watching is most often a solitary experience, though much time is spent on the phone comparing notes with friends and neighbors on the day's events in Soapland. Among fans, soaps are probably a more popular topic of conversation than the weather.

The day's events are planned around favorite shows. The phone is often taken from its hook, and heaven help the door-to-door salesman who tries to interrupt. Shopping, hair appointments, and trips to the dentist are scheduled accordingly. If something unavoidable or untoward keeps the fan away from her set, little time will pass before she calls an equally addicted friend to catch up on her stories.

She will, however, very seldom discuss them with her husband or children. It is as if the soaps were a secret education. One researcher called them a "secret weapon in the sex war," referring to the fact that to many fans the soaps are a how-to course for their domestic and marital lives. The soaps' role as teacher and guide is an important one. Interviewed about why they like soaps, fans say they teach "how to be with a husband," "how to handle problems with children," and "how to have romance."

In the days of radio soap, listeners claimed they learned

all kinds of important lessons from their favorite programs. One woman said that Papa David of *Life Can Be Beautiful* had taught her to be "more cheerful when Fred my husband comes home." She found *The Goldbergs* helpful, too. "Mr. Goldberg," she pointed out, "comes home scolding and he never means it. I sort of understand Fred better because of it."

Another woman admitted that she was trying to model herself after Helen Trent. As she said, "I like Helen Trent. She is a woman over thirty-five. You never hear of her dyeing her hair. She uses charm and manners to entice men and she does. If she can do it, why can't I? I am fighting old age, and having a terrible time. Sometimes I am tempted to go out and fix my hair. These stories give me courage and help me realize I have to accept it."

It seems plain that a large number of fans have always taken the soap and swallowed it whole. Such gullible dependency, such blind acceptance of the soap as truth, puts a heavy onus on the writers and producers.

In the same way that a comic book can help a beginner to learn words by associating them with the pictures, the daytime serial, which shows people living day-to-day lives with day-to-day problems, can help a viewer deal with hers. But just as a comic book can become an easy-to-take substitute for real reading, so a soap opera can, for some members of its audience, become a substitute for real life.

Their favorite soap opera heroine's daily life often parallels the viewers' own. The stories most often go day by day, Monday through Friday, corresponding to the days of the week on the real calendar. Holidays like Thanksgiving and Christmas are duly celebrated. An ingenuous viewer, or some part of her, can very easily confuse these make-believe events and characters with those in her own life.

Most viewers hold on to some sense of reality, only letting part of themselves become submerged in the substitute life presented to them. Others, however, get a little muddled. These are the viewers who accept the stories as real. They talk of them as real. Indeed, the places, characters, and events of the soaps fill their lives as if they were real. A half hour each day spent with Vanessa Sterling in close physical proximity, right there in one's own living room, often under intimate, confidential, and personal circumstances, and these viewers know her better than their best friend, and often better than their spouses.

Mary Stuart (Joanne of *Search for Tomorrow* for over twenty years, and the first soap opera actor to be nominated for an Emmy award) tells this story:

"They insist they know you. I had a lady come up to me in Bloomingdale's one day and she said, 'You never even wrote me a thank-you note.' And I said, 'Eh . . . eh . . . for what, madam?' She said, 'You came to my house for a party. We were selling that kitchenware, and you never even wrote me a thank-you note.'

"'Now, ma'am, I wasn't there. I know what you mean. I've kind of been in your living room. You do kind of know me.'

"'You were certainly there. I remember. You bought that nice kettle . . .'

"I said, 'I'm on television.' No. No way to convince her. I had had lunch with her. I'd been in her house. And that was that. She was furious and stalked off."

This line between fantasy and reality is an elusive one. Much of the mail that the producers receive speaks of the characters as real. Thousands and thousands of letters give advice, warn the heroine of impending doom, caution the innocent to beware of the nasties ("Can't you see that your brother-in-law is up to no good?"), inform one character of another's doings, or reprimand a character for unseemly behavior.

Perhaps the most baffled, baffling, and poignant of such letters was one sent to an actress who for years had played the part of a Broadway actress on a popular soap. The fan began by saying how much she liked the show, how she watched every day, and how much she enjoyed the actress's performance in the role of the Broadway star. Then she concluded the letter by asking, "Have you ever thought of becoming an actress in real life?"

Eileen Fulton, who plays Lisa Hughes, infamous goodie-baddie of *As the World Turns,* was approached one day by a well-turned-out matron who asked, "Are you Lisa Hughes?"

Smiling in expectation of an autograph request to follow, Miss Fulton admitted that she was. "Well," cried the stranger, as she administered a hard slap in the face, "I hate you!"

Of course, not all contacts between fan and actor take place in the shadowy zone between fantasy and reality. Any soap actor can tell you about encounters with his viewing public in broad daylight. Most often these chance meetings are in restaurants, in the subway, or on the street, and they are gratifying to the actor and exciting to the fan. Usually the fan will not know the actor's real name but say, "Aren't you so-and-so?" and the actor will say, "Yes, I am," and the fan will say, "I watch you all the time." This is satisfying to the actor, who thus discovers that somewhere out beyond the camera lens, out there somewhere, his work is being seen.

Contacts with the audience also have their less pleasant side. If you are appearing regularly on a soap, your life is barely your own. If your number is in the phone book, calls will come from all over the country at all times of day or night: "Hello." Giggle. "Is this Philip Holden?" More giggles. "Oh, my God, I got him. It's him! Is it really you?" At the risk of being considered a recluse or an ingrate, a soap opera regular must have his phone unlisted.

Travel, including walking in public places, takes courage. The use of a disguise such as dark glasses, slouch hat, and upturned collar allows your friends to accuse you of putting on airs, but sometimes it is the best defense. Being recognized is generally a nice thing and often a pleasant boost to the ego, but it can be a demoralizing experience.

The fan will ask defiantly, "You're Philip, aren't you?" She won't take no for an answer. There is no way to escape, since she is grasping your shirtfront. Fans sometimes get very possessive. You are not a human being. You are their property. You are being pummeled and squeezed, pinched and caressed like a melon on a fruit stand. Your graciousness is being put to the test, and you are saved only when your subway stop arrives and you can escape. The fan has proved to herself that, as she suspected all along, you are real. But it is not you, the actor, who is real, but that twenty-one-inch close-up called Philip, who visits her home on the magic box several times a week.

One lady approached David in a department store: "I recognize you! You're on a soap opera! I watch you all the time! Which one is it? *Guiding Light*?"

"No," replied David modestly, "I'm on—"

"No, no, don't tell me! Let's see. It must be *Search for Tomorrow*!"

"No, actually I'm on—"

"No, no, don't tell me. I know, *Secret Storm*!"

David, by now slightly embarrassed, as a crowd gathered to see what the commotion was about: "No, but that's close. I'm on—"

"*No*! Don't tell me. Is it . . . let's see . . . is it . . . ?"

Now anxious to conclude the session, David offered: "Actually I'm on *Love of Life*."

Fan, undaunted: "No, *that's* not it. Is it . . . ?"

In the course of David's three-year stint on *Love of Life,* only three out of hundreds who approached him in public places knew his real name. Those events were particularly gratifying because the viewers, unlike most, had gone beyond the character and had bothered to note the name of the actor playing the part. If you see one of your favorite characters on the bus or in the bank, feel free to talk to him. If you know his real name, that would make it even nicer.

When David toured the country in the National Company of the Broadway musical *Cabaret,* loud whispers often accompanied his first entrance as Ernst, the German friend of Sally Bowles. The whispers could be heard on the stage: "It's Philip, it's Philip!" Children who have been brought up on television and movies, and adults who are unused to theatergoing, tend to forget that the actors can hear the audience. They are accustomed to talking back to their television sets.

Soap followers as a rule have incredible memories, further

proof that the characters insinuate themselves thoroughly into their lives. David as Philip Holden had not been seen on *Love of Life* for nearly eight years when the snappy check-out teller at a supermarket near Stratford, Connecticut, said recently that she recognized him. "I remember you. Philip on *Love of Life*. You were the one that did . . . well, you know."

David commended her on her remarkable memory, but had to correct her, explaining that he was only *accused* of doing You Know. Could a play- or moviegoer immediately recognize the face of a character from a performance she had witnessed eight years before—especially the face of an actor whom she did not know and had not seen since? But if that actor is on a soap regularly, say twice a week for a period of three years, the ardent fan will have spent over 150 intense hours of her life with that character.

Like any addiction, watching soaps can be a heavy habit. If the viewer has one favorite, she is likely to have three. Few watch more than three regularly. Very few watch only one.

Fans are also fiercely loyal to their favorites. The networks are aware of this and schedule their shows accordingly. A new or less popular show will be scheduled immediately before or after an old favorite. It is also a matter of great concern for the networks which shows may be competing in the same time slot on the other networks. Scheduling is a very tricky business.

A show may survive only because it follows a strong one or has no competition on another channel. As you can tell from the scheduling in nighttime, where mortality rates are even higher, a show may go off the air only because it was unable to grab enough of the ratings from a long-standing popular success being shown on another network. A show's demise does not necessarily mean it was bad, only that it was not as popular as its competition. By the same token, a show may survive for years merely because it has no competition.

In the winter of 1973, Procter & Gamble, knowing that their shows, being among the most popular, were being used to support weaker or lower-rated shows, pulled a very smart power ploy. They insisted, by threatening to move their shows to another network, that all the P&G shows be scheduled in a block, without being interrupted by a soap produced by the network or some other independent producing organization. It's a free world and a competitive market. Why should they support another soap advertising products competing with their own? Why indeed? The ploy worked.

There is little doubt that this reshuffling of time schedules was largely responsible for the demise of *Love Is a Many Splendored Thing* and *Where the Heart Is*. They just couldn't survive the switch to new time slots.

CBS expected and got at least 35,000 letters protesting the cancellation of these shows. They were relegated to the water-over-the-dam department. Networks always receive lots of mail about changes in soap operas, when one actor is replaced by another, or when a character is "killed off" on a show.

If an actor is incapacitated because of illness or other calamity and there is a temporary unavoidable replacement, the announcer, nowadays, comes in to say, "Today the role of so-and-so will be played by so-and-so." This probably averts many attacks of high blood pressure among the viewers.

The cancellation of a day's episode in order to show some national event—such as an Apollo launching, a presidential funeral, or a Senate hearing—brings an avalanche of protest mail.

Some of the networks' mail is the usual fan mail requesting information about an actor. Some gives advice on plot or casting. One Mailgram from an irate viewer—perhaps an addict ready to kick the habit—proclaimed: THERE ARE NO REASONABLE PEOPLE WHO GET THEMSELVES INTO SUCH DISGUSTING SITUATIONS.

The major portion of the networks' mail regarding soaps could be classified as morality mail. Almost anything offends someone, and soap watchers are quick to complain. The mail attests to the fact that in spite of the sexual revolution and the rest of it, we are still a comparatively puritanical nation. Offenses include drinking, language, discussion of premarital sex, and unlawful cohabitation. The networks try to answer all these letters. The weekly intake of mail is tabulated, and a report is forwarded to at least twenty offices within the network, from the president on down. What they make of the information thus recorded is anybody's guess.

So we have seen how the networks and ad agencies spend a lot of money to find out who their audience is. We have looked at the rating system that tells them how big their audience is. And we have tried to give some idea as to why the audience finds the daytime form so attractive.

But the big question remains. Why are millions spent to discover the quantity, quality, and quirks of the audience? Why the daytime serial at all?

The big answer is that viewers are consumers. Market research proves that viewers buy. And that, dear reader, is the name of the game. Commercials fill 25 per cent of your viewing time.

Each half-hour show is written and performed in five scenes or "acts." The running time of those five scenes totals about twenty-two minutes. The other eight minutes are devoted to commercials. Most of these are national network commercials, but some are local and advertise products only to certain regions. They may be local products (a local chain of health spas or hamburger stands, for instance), or they may be commercials for a national product specifically geared to appeal to a local market (the lady plumber in a New York tenement vs. the lady plumber in an Iowa farmhouse, for instance).

Many soaps are entirely owned and produced by their sponsors. Procter & Gamble has invested heavily in the daytime serial almost from the beginning. These soaps advertise their owners' products, although they may sell some of their commercial time to other sponsors. How many millions of dollars' worth of Procter & Gamble products must the viewers buy in order to make it desirable for P&G to spend over thirty million dollars annually in advertising these products?

The products hawked are aimed at the average soap viewer. You won't see any razor blades or beer bottles, because the male soap viewer—though he exists—constitutes too small a proportion of the audience. The commercials are aimed at the woman viewer, the homemaker, the housewife who does the dishes and the laundry. These shows are not called soap operas for nothing. Suds, traditionally and still, cop the lion's share of all commercials. In one quarter of 1972, for example, 47 per cent of the commercials shown on soap operas advertised food and soap. In lesser percentages were drugs and medicine, then personal-hygiene products, hair products, and household furnishings.

The number and frequency of commercials are controlled by the Federal Communications Commission. If some of the commercial time is unsold, the audience is not treated to more of the drama, but will get public service announcements—Heart Fund spots, Smokey the Bear, or antismoking commercials.

One fairly accurate gauge of the popularity of a soap is the number of such messages. Although a certain number of such public service spots are required by the FCC, you can be sure that if there are many of them, the show is not selling like the proverbial hotcakes.

The popularity of each show, as discovered through audience surveys, ratings, and market research reports, determines what it will cost the sponsor to buy time on that program. In 1966 the highest-rated show, *As the World Turns* on CBS, got as high as $13,000 a minute, other shows at CBS averaging $9000 to $10,000 a minute of sponsored time. That year ABC got from $5000 to $6000 and NBC, then lagging, got $4000 tops. Four years earlier, when the average was between $2500 and $3200, *As the World Turns* was getting $5000 a minute.

Total investment in daytime TV in 1972 was well over $300 million, soap opera accounting for over half of that. Each daytime serial, for each week of five half-hour segments, is almost as costly to produce as a Broadway musical.

Since 1967 these production costs have remained almost constant. The audience since then has increased a whopping 23 per cent. This increase in audience size means that commercials reach more people for the same amount of money. With more people watching and production costs fairly steady, the cost to the sponsor for each thousand people he contacts has dropped 19 per cent since 1967, according to a five-year study made in 1972.

Soap opera is indeed a paying proposition. Often the durable successes that show handsome profits for the networks are a healthy source of support for the other programing, such as game shows and prime-time series, which sometimes have briefer lives and are much more vulnerable to vagaries in audience ratings. Some people in the industry go so far as to claim that soap opera accounts for 60 per cent of all network profits.

If eight minutes out of every thirty are devoted to commercial messages, the other twenty-two must keep the audience riveted to the set. It must be twenty-two minutes of affecting story and good acting, adhering closely to the proven successful soap opera formula. But it is the effectiveness of the commercials on the soap opera—how much of the sponsor's product the viewers buy—that determines a given program's longevity. The audience does have something to say about what it sees on the daytime TV screen. Its letters of praise or protest may be ignored by networks or producers, but it continues to cast the decisive vote at the local supermarket, where it buys—or does not buy—the sponsor's product. Ultimately, it is the audience as consumer, not the audience as critic, that dictates which soap operas will thrive and which will die.

Making Soaps

§

[*MADELEINE and DAVID are still at work in the office. Close-up of overflowing ashtray, indicating that they have been at it for some time.*]

MADELEINE: . . . and that's all there is to it. You've got to tell them—let it all out. They have a right to know. They've sat through all those commercials, they've kept Procter & Gamble in business, they've kept the Nielsen ratings and the network executives hopping . . . Tell them everything they've always wanted to know.

DAVID: And weren't afraid to ask. [*Laughs hysterically.*]

MADELEINE: Careful, buster, we can always have you drive your car into an abutment.

DAVID: Sorry. I don't know what's the matter with me lately.

MADELEINE: Come on, Dave. I can see the light at the end of the tunnel, the pot at the end of the rainbow, the moon over Miami, the—

DAVID: Mad, you're jumping. That's Thursday's script. The cue was "I don't know what's the matter with me lately."

MADELEINE: Oh, I'm sorry, I don't know what's the matter with me lately.

DAVID: That's my line.

MADELEINE: What's my line?

DAVID [*wryly*]: Writer?

MADELEINE: That's not funny. You're supposed to tell them all about how it's done. Now, what is the question that viewers most frequently ask you when they attack you in the subway?

DAVID: "May I have a quarter for a cup of coffee?"
MADELEINE: No, no.
DAVID: Oh, you mean "How do you learn all those lines?"
MADELEINE: Well, how do you?
DAVID: Well, okay. Here we go: everything you've always wanted to know about how soaps are made, but were afraid to ask . . .

How was it in the beginning?

You may well ask. No one, of course, knew that the daytime serial would grow to be a multimillion-dollar business with lights and cameras and color and elaborate filmed commercials. It all started with a writer, an actor or two, and a shabby room with a microphone, a small transmitter, and maybe a fellow who watched the dials.

That's all?

All. Everyone would get there maybe fifteen minutes before air time, read through the script once, and then do it. Just read the parts, letting the pages drop silently to the floor as the program proceeded. Then the actors would try to collect their five- or six-dollar fees and everyone would go home. The cleaning lady would sweep up the discarded script and no one was ever the wiser.

And that's why there are few extant early scripts?

Right. Then, as you know, things began to change over the years. The form jelled, the audience swelled. The daytime serial reached its peak in the late thirties in the heyday of that modern miracle, radio. Production was no longer haphazard. Network radio afforded the serial a national and devoted following.

And then came television?

Well, yes, but not so fast. It was invented, but, as you recall, not so many families had television sets until sometime after World War II. No one could accurately predict what television would become, and they certainly didn't know what direction the daytime serial would take. Around the time Radio City was being completed, the National Broadcasting Company showed off the model television studio that was part of its broadcasting center of the future.

Oh? What was it like?

It was a large circular room with scenery lining the walls. In the center of the studio was a round glass-enclosed booth with one camera on a tripod which could swivel from one set to the other. Technically, television was in its infancy. Cameras were bulky and cumbersome. Severe, hot lights were required. Techniques and conventions had to be invented, tested. Slowly, and often clumsily, the new form evolved. Today, over twenty years later, the TV soap opera has probably arrived at its most complete, sophisticated form.

I'm not afraid to ask. Tell me about it.

Well, all right. But you may not really want to know. You often ask, How do you memorize all those lines? or, How long do you rehearse? But when details are forthcoming you cringe from the knowledge, not wishing to destroy the magic, to expose the trick. Others, like us, believe that a thorough knowledge of the inner workings can only lead to expansion of one's appreciation. If you are one of those who would rather not have a straight answer to the question, Is there a Santa Claus?, then stop here.

Ready.

All right. A Day in the Life of a Soap Opera, and *you* are there. You are one of the actors, let's say, on *Love of Life*. You will be featured in a major story line for several months, or longer—who knows? Today you are going to arrive on the scene. You are nervous. How will the inhabitants of Rosehill receive you? How will *America* receive you, those three to five million people who are out there watching?

I'm not sure I can go through with this.

It's only pretend. You've got to keep remembering it's only

pretend. But before we send you into the rehearsal room and then the studio, it is important that you know who all those other people are.

What other people?

Starting at the top, there is the network executive in charge of all the daytime programing. He in turn is responsible to others in the executive hierarchy, up to the president. As an actor you will never see any of them. No fraternization. You may see a conservatively suited gentleman (or lady) in the studio occasionally. That is the producer. If you did not meet him during your audition and hiring process, you probably will never talk to him—unless, of course, you are fired. But don't think about that.

He is the one ultimately responsible for the success or failure of the show, and it is his head that will roll if the ratings droop. He is nervous, too.

How did he get to be a producer in the first place?

Thinking of becoming a producer, are you? Most probably he has come up through the ranks, starting as, say, a production assistant, floor manager, or gopher ("Hey, kid, gopher some coffee, willya?"). He should have theater sense, good business acumen, and an awareness of the public's desires. He may be his own boss, if he happens to "own" the show and have his own production company. He may be an employee hired by the advertising agency that packages the show for the sponsors who own the show. Or he may be an employee of a network that is producing the show itself.

In any case, he is in charge of the production. Production starts with the scripts. And the scripts start with someone who has the idea in the first place.

I'd like to be one of those. May I?

Well, you can try. Presentations for new serials are made to the networks all the time, and occasionally new soaps come on the air. Their chance of success is very slim, the public being addicted to their old favorites. Sometimes a new soap is a spin-off of an older, very successful one (*Somerset* from *Another World*) or of a film (*Love Is a Many Splendored Thing*). Or it can be an original idea. The network or sponsor sometimes wants a new serial to replace a waning one or to fill an empty time slot. Great care is exercised in selecting a new project, so the source is usually an established producer or writer with a good track record. Traditions are well established and this is no place for a pioneer. A new idea may be superficially innovative, but in the end it must adhere closely to the proven formula.

Well, okay. Can you get me a job as a writer?

You're on your own there. Besides, today, in this chapter, you're an actor and we're trying to get you through one day's shooting. If you'll just stop asking so many questions.

Sorry.

But we're glad you asked about writers.

If you laid all the scripts for one soap for one year end to end, you would have the equivalent of fifty-two three-act plays. That's a lot of words.

Most soaps have one head writer. He is directly responsible to the producer, and together they plot and plan the course of the story line. It is his name that appears once a week on the credit roll at the end of the show. Sometimes there are two head writers who work in close cooperation. They may be a husband-and-wife team. A head writer earns about three thousand dollars a week.

How can one person—or even two—turn out so many scripts?

They couldn't possibly write all the dialogue for every script. They may actually write one, two, or even three scripts a week, but they need assistant writers. The head writers make up a projected story line which plots the action at least six months ahead. Then they make up story breakdowns which outline the action and content of each scene for each day, usually a week at a time. It is from these detailed sketches that the ghost assistants write their dialogue. Actual scripts are prepared only two or three weeks before scheduled air time. After editing by the producer, rewriting by the authors, and re-editing by the producer, the actor usually gets the script into his hands a couple of days before the taping date.

What does a long story projection look like?

Here. This is the rough chronology set forth for *Love of Life* covering February 1962 through April 1963, projecting the story line over a year ahead. Roy Winsor, the creator, was then the producer, Joseph Hardy the associate producer and script editor, and Don Ettlinger the head writer.

LOVE OF LIFE, *Rough Chronology*

FEBRUARY '62

MURANO killed. RICK implicated in murder, must use alibi that JULIE MURANO spent night in his apartment. This makes for final breach with BARBARA, who to VIVIAN's pleasure and VAN and BRUCE's discomfort definitely decides on divorce and makes arrangements for Mexican divorce. RICK takes over running of Havana Club with JULIE as boss. LINK-TAMMY growing closer to marriage. DENTON, murderer of MURANO, caught. PHILIP HOLDEN reassured by real criminal being caught rather than injustice done to RICK. BARBARA leaves for Mexican divorce.

MARCH

Girl who was in love with PHILIP HOLDEN in mental hospital shows up in Rosehill. PHILIP, realizing how important that he not reject her, refuses to try and keep her appearance a secret. Because of girl JUDSON WILLIAMS learns of PHILIP's mental hospital background, demands his dismissal from Winfield job. BRUCE and VAN go to mat for him, BRUCE threatening to quit as headmaster if PHILIP is dismissed. BRUCE finally wins. BARBARA returns from Mexican divorce.

APRIL

LINK and TAMMY announce their engagement. TAMMY concerned about whether she'll make good housewife for LINK. Other doubts about age, etc. The dead MAGGIE's twin sister (AGGIE?) appears on the scene, moves into PORTERS' house. She seems exact replica of sweet MAGGIE and is constant reminder of her to LINK. BARB gets job at Winfield as secretary. Meets again with TONY, and gradual rapprochement seems to be in offing. VAN alone distrusts and dislikes MAGGIE's TWIN. BARBARA discovers she's preg but tells no one.

MAY

VAN sees that MAGGIE's TWIN is out to get LINK (and SANDY) and is making progress. TAMMY more and more insecure. BARBARA and PHILIP HOLDEN become friends out at Winfield. BARB tells VAN (and VIV?) about pregnancy. ALAN falls for girl in beatnik crowd, begins, to VAN's and BRUCE's despair, to go way out. Beard, pad, poetry, sex—the works.

JUNE

RICK, now running Havana Club and carrying on loveless affair with JULIE MURANO, learns of BARBARA's pregnancy (possibly through TAMMY in SALTZMAN's office), tries to patch up marriage for sake of unborn child, but to no avail. TAMMY, in face of competition from MAGGIE's TWIN, withdraws more and more. LINK believes she's cooling off; she believes he is. MAGGIE's TWIN does everything to widen breach, every day ingratiating herself more and more with LINK and SANDY. TAMMY refuses to take VAN's advice and fight. ALAN gets in deeper with beatnik set and beatnik girl, maybe gets job as waiter in poetry-coffee joint and moves out of house.

JULY

BARBARA refuses to marry TONY, but won't tell him why. He decides to leave Rosehill, anything to get away from this mysteriously bulging Circe. TAMMY gets offer for made-to-order part in upcoming Broadway play and is very tempted to accept because of LINK-MAGGIE's TWIN situation. PHILIP quietly falling in love with BARBARA.

AUGUST

TAMMY decides to accept part in play—tacit breaking of engagement with LINK, who is enamored of MAGGIE's TWIN. VAN tries to dissuade TAMMY from decision to go back to New York and give up LINK but without success. She is furious with LINK, who can't see MAGGIE's TWIN for what she is. ALAN wakes up to discover he has only been used by beatnik crowd, supplying the money, the car, etc. Off comes the beard and all pretensions. ALAN begins to look again in SANDY's direction.

SEPTEMBER

BARBARA has baby. RICK there but no reconciliation. TAMMY leaves for N.Y.C. to begin rehearsals. MAGGIE's TWIN sure she's got it made. PHILIP's closest friend from Army days, GLENN HAMILTON, arrives in Rosehill, gets job playing at Havana Club. GLENN, with all his smiling and great friendship, obviously (to audience) insincere and up to no good. TONY returns to Rosehill, discovers BARBARA refused to marry him because of her pregnancy. He still loves her and asks her to marry him.

OCTOBER

TAMMY opens in play and is tremendous hit, a bigger star than ever. LINK, through VAN's efforts, begins to see MAGGIE's TWIN for what she is. TONY and BARB get married, baby and all. PHILIP quietly hurt, but takes it calmly, if sadly. PHILIP and RICK strike up friendship through PHIL's friend GLENN, playing at Havana Club. RICK reaction to BARB's marriage very strong and he almost goes off deep end—of bar, that is.

NOVEMBER

Final break between LINK and MAGGIE's TWIN. LINK, urged

by VAN, goes to N.Y. to woo big star, TAMMY. TONY and BARB face marriage with little money and a squalling baby, RICK begins weekly visits to baby with resulting tensions between TONY and him, TONY and BARB. First young girl attacked and murdered in Rosehill. PHILIP very upset.

DECEMBER

TAMMY decides to give up career, come back to Rosehill, and marry LINK. More attacks on young girls. PHIL asking himself if he did it. Very shaken. "Friend" GLENN and Mrs. HOLDEN don't help. LINK very suspicious of PHIL, as is JUDSON WILLIAMS, etc. VAN, BRUCE, BARB, etc., stand by him, refuse to be panicked.

JANUARY '63

LINK and TAMMY marry. Attacks on girls stepped up. WILLIAMS uncovers info on original accusation of PHILIP as girl-attacker which sent him to mental hospital. Wants to throw him out of Winfield. All hell breaks loose with everyone yelling for PHILIP's scalp. BRUCE and VAN (and SANDY) staunchly loyal and believing in PHIL, whose doubts about himself are growing. Is he doing these things? GLENN, supposedly helping, only increases his own doubts. BARB and TONY marriage tougher and tougher. TONY loses his job at garage, has to borrow money from RICK, who is getting richer and richer, and colder and colder.

FEBRUARY

Trap set for girl-attacker and PHILIP inadvertently walks into it. (Probably GLENN finds out about trap and sees to it that PHIL walks into it. Maybe SANDY bait in trap.) WILLIAMS insists on PHIL quitting Winfield and BRUCE, pressured by public opinion, forced to give in. RICK gets suspicious of GLENN, PHIL's piano-playing friend. LINK and TAMMY set up housekeeping and TAMMY faced with problems of housewife for first time. But VAN helping her out. (LINK and TAMMY also involved in PHILIP controversy, as are VIV and HENRY.)

MARCH

PHILIP wants to leave town but BRUCE won't let him, because to leave is an admission of guilt. RICK comes to BRUCE with suspicions about GLENN. BRUCE starts detective work and discovers attacks on girls have broken out in whatever towns GLENN has been playing the piano. TONY going to pieces in marriage, depending more and more on RICK for financial support. RICK always a part of the picture because of his visits to his son. SANDY and ALAN now very much and very seriously in love and even thinking of marriage.

APRIL

BRUCE unmasks GLENN as attacker of girls and original committer of crime which sent PHIL to hospital. (GLENN in Rosehill to implicate PHILIP because he feared he was going to be found out for original crime, wanted to ensure PHILIP being thought guilty.) MEG, VAN's sister, arrives in Rosehill, broke, but VAN lets her take over real estate business. MEG is going to get into big-time development of outlying Rosehill which will get everyone in a mess.

MAY

Writer collapses.

I'm a fan of Love of Life *and I don't remember all that happening. Besides, Maggie's twin sister was called Kay, not Aggie.*

Right. This story outline was only a guidepost. Many things were changed, delayed, eliminated, over the months. And you're right, the evil twin sister of Maggie, the recently deceased wife of Link Porter, was called Kay. She was played by Joan Copeland, the very same lady who had played sweet Maggie. She had been very popular on the show, and when Maggie died of leukemia she was brought back to the airwaves as Maggie's twin. Remember that?

Evil characters are often gotten rid of when they are found out, and so it was with Kay. Joan Copeland may now be seen on *Search for Tomorrow* as Andrea, the interfering mother of Len Whiting, a part she has played for many years.

How is an actual script written from that broad outline?

Carefully. The head writer makes up an outline for each day's script. Here is one of those daily breakdowns, as they are called, Episode No. 2919, dated Thursday, November 29, 1962. The characters used and the sets required are listed at the top, then each of the five "acts" with the action each is to contain.

LOVE OF LIFE

THURSDAY, NOV. 29th   CAST: PHIL, RICK, JULIE,
                              MRS. HOLDEN, CLYDE (5)
(#2919)   SETS: PORTER *kitchen,* RICK'S *office,*
                              PHIL'S *room*

ACT ONE

Phil comes home from Winfield to his room and his mother comes up with letter for him. From the return address she knows it's from his old Army buddy, Glenn Sanders—the one man who really befriended Phil when he had all the trouble. Phil happily opens the letter. Glenn has traced him through his aunt and uncle, wants to come to Rosehill, wants to know if there is any kind of a night spot where he might get a job playing the piano (his profession). Mrs. Holden all for discouraging Glenn's visit. He knows what no one besides Mrs. H. and Phil knows. Glenn Sanders knows the reason Phil was put in the mental hospital, the crime he was accused of. It should be forgotten. Mrs. H. is against anyone who knows that coming to Rosehill, but Phil, his nerves in a bad way, reminds his mother that he was innocent, that he is not going to live like a guilty criminal, and if Glenn needs help, he, Phil, certainly after all Glenn did for him, is going to give it to him. He's going out and talk to Rick Latimer.

ACT TWO

Rick is making arrangements to drive down to New York the next day for Tammy's opening when Julie comes in, hears of the plans, and insists that he take her. Rick doesn't want to. He doesn't like the increasing demands Julie makes on him. They have nasty argument in which Rick makes it clear that he owes Julie nothing, that their relationship is at her wish, not his, and that anytime she wants to end it, she can.

PROLOGUE

Later Julie is at the bar getting loaded and complaining of the miseries of love to Clyde when Phil comes in search of Rick. Julie eyes him with a jaundiced eye. Any friend of Rick's is no friend of hers.

ACT THREE

Rick comes out, sees Phil, who talks to him about possibility of a job for his friend, Glenn. Rick says he's been thinking of putting in a piano in the bar and if man is as good as Phil says he is he'll hire him. Scene is played against bitter comments from Julie. When Kay is mentioned and her departure from scene, Julie rises to her defense. What made Kay like she was? Men. That's the trouble with women. Men. Men and women's pathetic need for love.

EPILOGUE

Mrs. Holden is waiting for Phil when he gets home, pleading with him to write Glenn that there is no chance of a job for him here. She feels very strongly his coming will mean trouble—terrible trouble if the truth about Philip ever got out. Phil in a rage tells his mother he's going to write Glenn to come to Rosehill tonight.

I see that the projection had Glenn arriving in September and here it is the end of November and he hasn't gotten to Rosehill yet.

We told you they don't always hold rigidly to the story line. And not only that, but the script may turn out to be quite different from the breakdown, as a result of conversations between the head writer and that day's ghost assistant.

Are you going to show me a real script or not?

Yes, here is a scene from the actual script that was shown live on November 28 (you see, they even changed the date). The actors were David Rounds as Philip, Jessica Walter as Julie, and Barry Grael as Clyde, the bartender.

LOVE OF LIFE

PROLOGUE, From Episode #2919
Fade in:
Havana Club bar—an hour later

[CLYDE *is behind bar.* JULIE, *quite high, is at one end of bar. There are other customers but* CLYDE *is paying attention to* JULIE.]

JULIE: Another drink, Clyde. In fact, why don't you make it double and save yourself a little work.

CLYDE: You're really trying to tie one on tonight, aren't you? That must have been quite an argument you two had.

JULIE: Ah, love! That's what makes the world go round, isn't it, Clyde? And if you can't get love—liquor makes it go round too. [*Pause.*] You know, Clyde . . . I think I've finally figured it out.

CLYDE: What?

JULIE: The answer to the riddle . . . you know what I think? I think Rick is still carrying a torch for that ice-cold little nothing . . .

CLYDE: If that's true they wouldn't have got divorced.

JULIE: But maybe that divorce was just legal . . . divorces have to be made in heaven too, you know, Clyde, just as much as marriages do.

[*As* CLYDE *is considering this,* PHIL HOLDEN *enters.*]

PHIL: [*to* CLYDE]: Excuse me—can you tell me where I can find Rick Latimer?

CLYDE: Is he expecting you?

PHIL: No.

CLYDE: Then maybe you better call him and make an appointment. Is it business or personal?

PHIL: Well, business, I guess. But I am a friend of his.

JULIE [*interested*]: You a friend of Rick's? I never saw you before. I'm his partner—business partner.

PHIL: Oh—you're Julie Murano.

JULIE: Something tells me you've heard of me. That awful Julie Murano—who has such a bad reputation . . . Well, what did you want?

PHIL [*unwilling to talk to her*]: I'd better come back another time.

JULIE: Oh, go ahead and tell me what you wanted—I'll give Rick a message from you.

PHIL: Just say Phil Holden was here. [*Starts away.*]

JULIE: Phil Holden . . . where do I know that name from? Oh, yes . . . I know . . . you're the one who lives at Link Porter's house—right?

PHIL: Yes.

JULIE: You work out at Winfield Academy as a something or other . . .

PHIL: Librarian.

JULIE: And you . . . let's see now . . . what else do I know? Oh, of course—you're madly in love with Barbara Sterling. Clyde and I were just discussing her, weren't we, Clyde?

PHIL [*uncomfortable*]: Well, would you tell Rick I was here . . .

JULIE: Clyde—bring this gentleman a drink on the house. A Pink Lady. [*To* PHIL.] That'll remind you of Barbara, won't it? She and I went to school together, did you know that? True. I know her very well . . . very well indeed.

PHIL [*to* CLYDE]: Never mind the drink. I'm just leaving.

JULIE: Don't go. Any friend of Barbara's is . . . Well, any friend of Barbara's is someone I'm ready to sympathize with. And besides, there was some reason I wanted to meet you . . . something else I heard about you, but I've forgotten what it was. Something you've done is very unusual . . . what in the world was it?

PHIL: I was in a mental hospital. Is that what you mean?

JULIE [*sobered*]: I'm sorry . . . I'm very sorry. Look—you want to see Rick—well, I'll take you up to his office. You won't need any appointment if you come with me.

[*Fade out.*]

Now that I have the script, what do I do with it? I mean, what does the actor do with it?

He will read it and if he has any sense at all he will try to learn it. When you get into rehearsal you'll see how important it is to have some grasp of the words before rehearsal starts, because after that you will have very little time for such things. If you are not a "quick study" you will soon figure out how to be one. If you are on the show three, four, or maybe even five times a week, you will have to learn how to memorize quickly.

What if I forget the lines?

The director will be mad at you. You will be extremely unhappy and embarrassed. Your face will turn crimson and you will probably stammer incoherently. In short, you will make an ass of yourself.

Or, if you can keep your head while all about you are losing theirs, you can surreptitiously glance at the teleprompter.

What is a teleprompter?

Ah! It is a machine mounted on a camera. It holds a roll of yellow paper on which has been typed, in fairly large print, the script of the day. One of these machines is mounted on the side of each camera. An operator controls the progression of the rolls from a remote part of the studio. And if you, the actor, suddenly say to yourself, "Oh, my goodness, I don't know what my next line is," then you look casually around to find one of the prompters whose little arrow will be pointing at the words on the roll that you are supposed to say next.

Is that all there is to it?

No. Lesson No. 1: Don't depend on the teleprompter. The prompter itself is reliable enough, but there is an art to using it. First, you must be cool-headed enough to search for your words nonchalantly, so that America will not stop its ironing and say, "Oh, look at the dumb actor, he forgot his words." Second, your characterization must be strong enough and your concentration secure enough so that while you are looking around for the words you don't forget whatever else you're supposed to be doing. Third, time is of the essence. The clock and the cameras keep moving relentlessly.

Did David, during his tenure on Love of Life, *become proficient in the use of the teleprompter?*

Don't ask. David reports that the first time he realized that he had more to say but could not think of the words, he found himself gaping helplessly at the accusing lens of the live camera. He was rescued by the next actor, cued on early to save the day. He resolved that the next time the lines escaped him he would have more control and extricate himself from his word-lessness with aplomb. Some weeks later such an occasion presented itself. With supreme confidence he turned casually to a camera that he knew was not "on."

Not "on"? What good would that do?

That means not broadcasting at that particular moment. If you look at the camera that *is* on (the one with the little red light on top), you will be looking right out at America and everyone will know that you blew it.

That's not good, is it?

No. So David turned ever so casually to that other camera, only to discover that although the camera itself was plainly in view the prompter attached to it was entirely hidden behind a piece of furniture. So there was no help for it. He just took half a second to think and the words came back to him. This is the best way to act anyway, if you can swing it. Know the lines.

If there are obvious goofs can't they just stop and start over?

No, no. That would cost money.

Who is this director you mentioned before?

He's the Man. When it gets to rehearsal and production in the studio, he's the boss. And no, in anticipation of your next question, you do not want to be a director, unless you have the artistic finesse of Laurence Olivier, the technical knowledge of Hammacher Schlemmer, and the nerves of a sky-diver.

They say that the best artistic work is done under the most stringent of rules, the most restricting conventions. In soaps you've got all that and more. You've got the strict soap opera form refined to an exact and exacting formula; you've got the burden of depending on six or eight fallible actors and perhaps fifty not infallible technicians, and enough cables, tubes, and transmitters to choke a horse.

Of all the communications media, none is so immediate as "live" radio or television, or so irrevocable. What you hear and see is happening at that very moment. It will never be heard again. Like stage plays or films, soap operas are planned, written, and rehearsed; but unlike them, once they are performed, that's it. There's no going back to the drawing board, or trying again another time for another audience. The die is cast (or the cast is dead) and there is no turning back.

In the nineteen-fifties, the so-called Golden Age of Television, before the advent of videotape recording, most TV drama was live, including the daytime serials. You, at home, saw exactly what the camera was seeing at that very moment. Nighttime television soon went to tape and then mostly to film. For financial reasons, the soaps did not immediately follow this trend. Tape was expensive.

Two soaps (*The Edge of Night* and *As the World Turns*) are still broadcast live. The rest are "live tape," which means that they are recorded straight through without stopping, as if they were being shown live. The advantage is that if there is a major mishap the tape can be stopped and the error redone or subsequently edited out. Editing is expensive, so the networks are loath to do it. Minor mistakes are left in on the theory that most people won't notice, and even if they do it won't hurt. So for all intents and purposes the soaps are live.

The director is the one who must maintain at least an illusion of being in complete and comfortable control. He must display endearing leadership qualities and keep his calm through the most harrowing and pressing times. He may laugh his way to the bank, since he is probably making something over two thousand dollars a week, but he must be sure to save enough to pay for pacifying his ulcerated stomach and shattered nerves.

Who else should I know about?

Well, since you already have the job, you have already met the casting director, a job given exclusively to women, apparently.

What is the reason for that?

We were just going to ask you the same question. In any case, your agent has submitted you for a part that has come up, and maybe sent over a picture. If the producer or casting person is familiar with your work from the stage or other television, you will have a head start. If the role is to be a sustained one, rather than a walk-on or under-five (a part with less than five speaking lines), you will, if the casting person thinks you are a likely candidate, read for the producer, who generally has the final word on casting. If it is a pivotal role, you may be auditioned on camera in the studio, perhaps with one of the other actors with whom you may be scheduled to play. That way they get to see what you look like on the screen and how you look next to the other actors.

How will I be able to stop shaking?

You probably won't. What they will be looking for is some assurance and security in what you do. So fake it. Act it. Confidence and relaxation are half of what acting is, anyway.

What else will they be looking for?

Probably a WASP type, so if you are one, terrific. Ethnic types are still rare on daytime. If they want a Negro, don't be too black. Italian? Just a trace. Jewish? Don't look it. Dress clean and conservative. When you read, grasp the sense of the scene in your head, relax, say the words sensibly and directly to the other actor, take your time, stay open for easy reactions to what he will say to you. Reaction is just as important as action. Listen. Think. Don't read your next line until you know what you're going to say. Speed counts for nothing. If they are good casters they will look for this open, relaxed interplay of minds and hearts, since this is what the best of soap depends on and is about. Do not worry about facial expressions, hand gestures, or movement. If something is happening in your head, the camera will see it.

And then they hire you?

Then you go home and wait. You anxiously recap your reading and decide where you did badly. You call your agent and report. Then you sit and hope for the call from him that just might say they want you.

Do they?

For the purposes of this chapter, yes. Don't let it go to your head.

What happens next?

After prolonged bickering with the producer, during which the terms of the contract are determined, your agent will have you sign something that says you are guaranteed one or two shows each week, that you are bound to them for two or three years, and that you will be paid somewhere from $187 to $350 for each show. The agent, by agreement with your union, the American Federation of Television and Radio Artists, will collect 10 per cent of that from you.

Of course, this contract does not guarantee you two or three years' work. They can fire you at the end of any cycle (thirteen-week period). Or the show can go off the air, in which case the producer and all are out of work too. But, all things being equal, *you* are bound to *them* for the period of the contract. The contract often stipulates, though, that you may—if you ask sweetly and with adequate warning—be released (or written out, as they say) for a period of four weeks for the purpose of making a film or appearing in a Broadway play.

Why would I want to do that?

To further your career, oddly enough.

But on a soap I'll be seen by millions of people and be making good money. Isn't that enough? What more could an actor want?

A little respect. For some unknown and largely invalid reason, the theater world does not rate a soap opera actor anywhere near the top of the stardom scale. Mary Stuart is not the star: Joanne Tate is. Not Audrey Peters: Vanessa Sterling! The public sees it that way, and the show business world is similarly narrow. It is a rare, if not extinct, movie or theater bird who will watch soaps with the idea of scouting talent.

Isn't that too bad?

That is too bad. Many top-quality actors appear on soaps. Good acting is one of the soaps' best attributes and one reason for their durable success. The relative security of a constant income is terribly attractive to any actor. This is one reason why many of the best appear.

What other reasons are there?

They can learn a lot about acting. If they have trouble with concentration, production circumstances will necessitate it. If they are slow learners, they will soon, with enforced practice, become quick studies. The Learning-to-swim-by-throwing-into-deep-water School of Drama.

You quickly learn how to play yourself, because basically, after the first few weeks, when the directors, writers, and producer have seen your work, the character is made to fit you. You will have problems that are not your own—alcoholism, amnesia, or whatever—but it will be *you* having those problems. So there is usually very little "character" work to do. Ergo, no façade for the actor himself to hide behind. It really must, according to the emotional demands made by the script, all hang out.

Won't I get bored doing the same thing day after day?

Probably. But it's not like, say, a long run in a Broadway play where you say the same things night after night and it becomes relentlessly and increasingly more difficult to keep it fresh. On soaps you get to say new words every day. And your character continues to develop, sometimes over a period of years.

One exception: because not all the audience is watching every day, it is often necessary to recapitulate the action of previous days. So important scenes must be repeated at least three times so the audience can catch up. It isn't exactly the same scene, of course. If it took place last time over coffee at the kitchen table, it will be in the living room next time. The dialogue will be slightly different, too, which makes it difficult to learn. You keep thinking, Gee, I've said all this before.

Such awkward repetition of the antecedent action is undesirable, of course, and better writers avoid it or use other techniques to keep the audience up to date.

What do they do instead?

In the olden, golden days of radio, the popular accepted method was the use of a narrator who used up several minutes of the program filling the audience in on the past. This technique obsolesced fast with the transfer to television. It began to seem awkward and old-fashioned—but it certainly was useful.

I repeat, what do they do instead?

The advent of certain technical improvements, such as sound and videotape, allows more freedom. Sometimes a section of a previously taped scene is simply repeated at the beginning of the following show. Or there's a flashback where a character thinks back in his mind to an earlier event and, zap, a fuzzy segue, and there we see it again. Another way to avoid having unrealistic, repetitive dialogue in order to get the exposition out is to have a monologue. This is an old trick but a goody, if not overused. This is where an actor thinks while a pretaped voice (his own) is played. You've seen a lot of that one.

Aren't you getting off the track?

Yes. But you should know some of the tricks and traps before you get into it. Most directors and producers do not consider the scripts inviolable, so you may be able to change a few lines in rehearsal. This may seem sacrilegious, but it is you who will have to say the lines and there are occasions when the director will let you change a word here and there to make it sound more natural. Certain writing gimmicks will begin to irritate your sensibilities after a time.

Like what?

One of the most overused devices is an easy way to end a scene when the writer can't think of another way out. That is to repeat a line, any line. "I don't know what I'm going to do. I just don't know what I'm going to do." Or, poignantly, "We'll see . . . we'll see." If the director likes you and you do not fear losing your job, always try to get them to cut half of any such line. America will thank you.

I am champing at my bit. May I go to rehearsal now?

Are you ready?

Am I?

Do you know what a P.A. does?

I'm the one who's supposed to ask the questions. What does a P.A. do?

A P.A. (production assistant) is a person, usually a girl, who assists the director during rehearsal and show. She can be identified because she has a stopwatch ostentatiously hanging around her neck. Her main job is to keep track of the time. At the first read-through she will time the scenes as the actors read through the script. The first, clumsy reading will give a surprisingly accurate indication of how long the scene will actually run on the air. If it is short or long, this is when it will be cropped or padded with additional dialogue or business.

Each time the scene is rehearsed, the P.A. will time it, marking in her script where the clock is at various points throughout the scene. In the later rehearsals and during the actual show she will know whether the scene is proceeding at the proper predicted speed. Her constant reports to the director will keep him informed on whether the show is "under," "over," or "on the nose."

If the show looks long, the director can signal the actors through the floor manager (stage manager) to speed up, talk a little faster. This may happen between scenes or during the commercial, or perhaps you, the actor, may see the floor manager signaling you to speed up by making a circular motion with his finger. If the show is under, he may signal you to stretch things by drawing his hands apart as if pulling taffy. It takes a cool-headed and experienced actor to retain control under such unesthetic instruction.

Does this sort of thing go on all the time?

No, but occasionally. Unpredictable things can happen on the air to change the timing of a show. The actors can get emotionally involved in what they are doing and may play the scene fuller then they did in rehearsal. Or they may skip lines, thereby putting the scene under. But it is essential that the director get it all back on the track. Commercials must be on schedule. If a show runs long and cuts into a commercial's time, there will be hell to pay.

What other ways can a director control the time?

He can go to black (fade out) at the end of a scene quickly and thus gain a couple of seconds. Or he can hold a close-up on one of the actors for many seconds before fading out. This will add time if he needs to stretch. As an actor you must keep on acting up a storm until you see the stage manager wave his script as a signal that the scene is over.

The most adjustable time period is at the end, when the credit roll is shown. If time is short, the roll will roll very fast indeed. If more time is needed, the credits will crawl across the screen. Most unions require that the names of the actors, production staff, technical staff, and so forth, be credited at least once a week. If things are really desperate, the scheduled credits may be postponed to another day.

In extremis, dialogue can be cut or stage business added at the last minute. John Desmond once had Mary Kaye Stone do a little tap dance to fill up some extra time on *Love Is a Many Splendored Thing.* Fortunately it was appropriate to both scene and character. And luckily the actress could dance.

Is there anything else I should know?

Plenty. But you have so much to cope with on your first day on the show that it's probably better just to put on your blinders and concentrate on your own job. Remember, you're supposed to be an actor.

Doesn't that remind you of an anecdote?

Yes. An actor was complaining to his psychiatrist. "Doctor, I don't know what to do. This business is impossible. I'm so frustrated. I can't act. I can't sing. I can't dance." PSYCHIATRIST: "Why don't you give it up and try something else?" DISTRESSED ACTOR: "I can't. I'm a star!"

Very funny.

Thank you. Now, pay attention, actor. You are about to hear what your first day on a soap will be like.

It is time to show up at the rehearsal room. You go to a small top room, several stairways up in Liederkranz Hall. This was the studio on East Fifty-eighth Street, now razed, from which *Search for Tomorrow* and *Love of Life* emanated for many years, before the advent of color and the building of the large CBS production center on West Fifty-seventh Street. It was (or is, since you are entering it now) a charming old building, erected as a concert hall decades ago, reputed to have had superb acoustics, but it has become a television studio.

And this is your rehearsal room. A room like any other room. Perhaps larger and crummier than some. There are a couple of dozen folding chairs scattered about. A folding table or two. One director, one production assistant, and six actors. They are Vanessa Sterling, Bruce Sterling, Link Porter, Tammy Forrest, Sandy Porter, and your mother, Mrs. Holden. They don't know you, but you know them. You've been watching *Love of Life*.

They look up from their sandwiches and coffee and greet you warmly as introductions are made all around. They chat and joke and reminisce about that day's show, aired just an hour before. And here they go again, ready to rehearse the episode that will air the next day at noon. At that time yours will be added to the gallery of faces that flicker through America's living rooms.

You feel the way you did when you were transferred to another school. What will the kids think of you, the stranger, the interloper? Make the new boy cry. Your trepidations are quickly eased as each welcomes you heartily to the club. My goodness, you think, these people are just as nice as their characters, and very much like them. The ambience is friendly and casual. Maybe everything is going to be all right.

Larry Auerbach, spelled only occasionally by an assistant, has directed *Love of Life* since its premiere on September 24, 1951. Here it is 1963. In 1973 he will still be directing this second oldest extant television soap. To endure and thrive in this job he must have a soft heart, a quick brain, and steely nerves. As you quickly discover, he does.

But things suddenly turn serious. It's time to read through the script. The others open their fresh white pages. You open your dog-eared copy. The words you have been studying for days on buses and elevators, in daydreams and nightmares, suddenly look new and foreign. You croak your first line. That's not your voice, you think. What will Larry (you are already on a first-name basis) and the others think? It's too late to find another actor for tomorrow's show. Or is it?

They have really socked it to you. You are in every scene. Five out of five. It is not an easy initiation. But you are going to be a major character. You (Philip Holden) have been talked about for weeks. Vanessa and Bruce, Link and Tammy and Sandy, and your mother, all are anticipating with anxiety your arrival in Rosehill. America is waiting.

The script is read and each scene timed. Then the script is discussed. "What does this mean?" "What does that mean?" "Am I going to marry him?" "How do I know that he is planning to do that?" "Why don't I see that he doesn't believe me?"

The actors know what's to become of them only a week or so in advance. They learn it from their scripts, which arrive in the mail a week or less before the show date. Although the long story projection outlines what is to happen to each character, the actors are seldom told. They live their soap lives from day to day, simultaneously with the viewers.

Sometimes the veteran actors will know their characters better than the writer does. Inconsistencies occur because of the assembly-line process with head writers and their ghostly helpers, and errors slip into the script. Or perhaps there has been a change in writers and the current one does not know the entire character history. An actor who has been with the show for years can set things straight during rehearsal.

Other discussions may be more philosophical, psychological, or esthetic. "Oh, Larry, I don't think Vanessa would say that, not that way. She's too nice a person." Or: "Oh, do I have to say that? It's so soapy. Can't I just nod or roll my eyes instead?"

Larry, with the author's and producer's tacit approval, often allows small script changes during the rehearsal process. It is important that the actors feel at ease with the script, that the dialogue appear natural.

The script approved by the actors, it is time to put it "on its feet." Tables and chairs are moved around to form the various sets. This is the Porter kitchen, this the Sterling living room. You transfer, in your mind's eye, what you remember from your home TV screen. Oh, yeah, the Porter kitchen: the table's here, the back door's there. Here it is in the flesh—or, rather, in skeletal form. You will drink more morning coffee in this kitchen in the next three years than you can shake a stick at.

Everything seems jovial and casual, belying the fact that you have reached the point of no return. The clock has started, and by 12:30 the next afternoon this, your virgin appearance, will be over with, for better or for worse.

You put the first scene on its feet, making the moves and doing the stage business required by the script. Suddenly it seems you do not know one of the words you have so diligently studied. You were, as they say in the theater, "bedroom-perfect," which means that you knew the lines perfectly well at home alone, but now they have gone clean out of your head. But they'll come back to you and all will be well, Larry and the others assure you.

Larry Auerbach's technique is to let the actor find the natural moves in the scene for himself. He then goes home and figures out how he will utilize the three cameras he has to work with in shooting the scene. There is no feeling of playing to this camera or that. In fact, he makes a point of not letting you know which camera is "on" or what is being shot at any particular moment.

Each scene is rehearsed maybe three or four times, and lo, you discover that you remember some of the words after all. The atmosphere in this ascetic rehearsal room is lighthearted, bordering on the festive. There is much wit thrown about, interjected into the more serious business at hand. Everyone's attitude toward the material is slightly irreverent, but underneath you find an abiding respect and seriousness. This is your family, after all, the Sterlings, the Porters, the Holdens, and you already feel a camaraderie and a closeness. You are all in the same boat, this life raft.

You leave the rehearsal after three hours of this preliminary indoctrination. You are experiencing a warm glow. Everybody was terrific and you weren't bad yourself. All will be well.

Now, what to do with the next twelve hours before you are due to show up again in the studio itself? The studio itself! Once again the gnawing panic. It will be months of doing this regularly before your nervous system will be anywhere near what you might call normal. In fact, you will not remember what normal was.

How to spend the evening? Studying the script? It is almost in shreds already, suffering from overuse. Have a large dinner? Perish the thought. Take in a movie? Forget it. Watch television? Shudder.

You find you have worried yourself through till bedtime. Bedtime! Sleep at a time like this? You are going to need your strength, you keep saying to yourself. So bed it is, where you lie counting, not sheep but the minutes that creep slowly into hours as you mark the time before heading back to the soap factory. You have set the alarm for 5:30, the middle of the night, but you have to be there at 7:15.

At 5:25 you turn off the alarm. Your internal clock has been working overtime. It will be months before you will sleep deeply enough to let the alarm perform its assigned task. You bound into action, exhilarated with anticipation, half sick with excitement. This is it! Clang, clang! Battle stations.

How beautiful and still New York is at 6:30 in the morning. The streets glisten from a nighttime shower. The sun, why yes, there it is coming up over Long Island City, a red ball at the east end of Fifty-seventh Street luring you to triumph or disaster. The bus is occupied by two cleaning ladies, traveling homeward after their day's night work. It is tempting: "Excuse me, ladies, but you might be interested to know that I'm making my debut on *Love of Life* today and if you'd care to watch . . ." You tamp the temptation.

You're back in the rehearsal room again. A table is set up with a coffee urn and breakfast buns, à la American Red Cross sending the boys to the battlefield. The morning run-through goes steadily if groggily. Larry seems pleased. You have remembered all your words.

Then you go downstairs to the studio for FAX, which means facilities, to block in the show on the sets with microphones and cameras. For the next two hours things are agonizingly slow. A jumble of cables, cameras, microphones on booms, lights being adjusted and getting hotter by the minute, furniture being moved, and props being placed. You are a racehorse, bred for this event, now warming up in the paddock, champing at your bit. Let's get on with it. What will the results be? Win, place, or show? Pull yourself together or it may be scratch.

Since you are in every scene this first day, you are required on the studio floor every minute. You wonder if this is a premeditated plot to keep you busy so you won't have time to contemplate your panic button. The plot fails. Your internal clock is ticking, clacking rather like Big Ben.

You have been told to wear a suit, so you have brought your suit, which you now don. You hope it looks all right. You should have had it pressed. Too late.

Every hour or so you have a few minutes of rest, at which time you are sent to makeup. There a lady with magic fingers will make you feel moderately acceptable in appearance. She wipes you with a pancake base, then "narrows" your nose by shading it on the sides. You begin to feel very unhappy with your God-given nose and a little ashamed that a cosmetic correction is deemed necessary, but then you find out that she does it to everybody, since the harsh lights tend to widen and flatten your features. More dark shading is put on your eyelids, as the lights otherwise would exaggerate them. A modest darkening of the eyebrows, lick your lips, just a touch of mascara—you don't want to look like Valentino as the Sheik—and you are ready for dress rehearsal. Since you are very "heavy" on the show this first day (that means you have a lot to do—see how quickly you pick up the jargon?), it has taken you five trips to the makeup room to get it done. Just as she gets to your left eye you are called back to the set, where, with Kleenex stuffed around your neck to protect your costume, you pick up Philip Holden where you left him off.

The sets, usually three per episode, are placed around the studio. Gee, they look funny. You had no idea. This is 1963 and color has not yet invaded daytime serials, so the sets—why is this surprising?—are gray and black. More than that, there are no walls where you thought there were walls. This, you learn, was an ingenious conception of Roy Winsor, your producer, who created this production technique used on the two shows he then produced for American Home Products, *Love of Life* and *The Secret Storm*. Every room in Rosehill, you now realize, has gray wooden wainscoting and chair rail. Above this paneling there is a black velour wall or—what?—no wall at all! A tall piece of furniture may be placed in front of this "wall" or a picture hung from the studio ceiling, and voilà! a wall seems to be there. A trick of the camera eye and a logical assumption by the viewer. This not only provides for sensible economy, but cleverly allows a camera to roll behind one of these "walls" and shoot the action over the wainscoting. Of course color made this technique instantly obsolete, but it worked well for the first fourteen years of *Love of Life*.

You creak through each scene while seemingly insurmountable technical complications are worked out. There is no way to get a microphone near you without casting a huge shadow from the mike boom across your face; camera two's cable becomes tangled around the kitchen table; camera three can see camera one peeking around the grandfather clock. Time out to fix this and that. But this is not a game; the clock does not stop for time-outs.

FAX is over and you get a half-hour break before the dress rehearsal. A quick sandwich and a container of milk. You check the script for the 1200th time. You get powdered down by the makeup artist. You comb your hair yet again.

Back on the set, and the words and the hundreds of other things you have to remember are rattling around somewhere behind your eyes. You even wonder what you look like since you became Philip Holden. Larry prohibits any monitors (TV receivers) on the set. This is so you can't sneak a side glance to check out how you look. Just act.

The dress rehearsal has started, in every way like the real thing that looms closer, more ominously imminent with each tick of the clock. Things are getting serious now. There is very little levity. The floor manager gives you a ten-second warning, then five, then counts silently, waving his script in your line of vision when the "go" moment is reached. The teleprompters are now mounted on the cameras, glaring the words in your face. They seem not so much dependable helpers as Big Brothers watching your every move to catch your tiniest error.

The organist is there, too, and the familiar *Love of Life* theme fills the studio. He is following the script and a monitor and improvises frills and "stings" to accentuate the emotion of the moment. You wait between scenes while the commercials are interpolated. The stage manager is waving at you again, and once more you find yourself moving, talking, gesticulating, like some efficient robot, programed by six hours of rehearsal.

Then you hear the announcer, Ken Roberts, pronounce the tag: "This has been *Love of Life*." My goodness, it must be over! But wait a minute . . . in half an hour we do it again, this time for real.

Larry seems pleased. "That was terrific, fine." Is he talking to you? He's talking to you! But we have to cut twenty seconds out of act two, rehearse a couple of actor-camera traffic jams. There seems to be something technical wrong with camera three, so they set about fixing that. The prop men are running around with paintbrushes, patching scratches on the set and furniture, spraying dulling wax on this doorknob and that picture frame so they won't glare in America's eyes.

You return to your script, remembering that hideous moment when you paused in the third act and all you could think of was, "You ding-dong! You don't know your next line!" Then the dread call: "Five minutes, everybody." The point of no return.

Your interior dialogue begins: What's to worry about? It's only a TV show, only a soap opera. Five years from now, no one will remember today, the day you made a complete ass of yourself in front of America. No, really, in the scheme of things it's not important, like putting a man on the moon, or the election of a President, or opening in a Broadway play, or being on a soap opera . . . Oh, Lord, this *is* a soap opera! You've got a job on a soap opera. You've hoped and trained for this job for years, and here you are. Isn't this exciting? Isn't this petrifying? No, no! Minimize, minimize. It's nothing, just another day, a speck in time, significant to no one. I'm ready. Casual, cool, in complete control.

"Stand by, thirty seconds!" The fuse is lit.

A kindly veteran stagehand, noticing your anxiety, attempts to soothe your impending hysteria. "What's a matter, kid? Don't be nervous." You smile weakly and nod your appreciation for his concern. He continues: "Just remember, more people are watching you today than saw Sarah Bernhardt in her entire career!"

DAVID: Have another cup of coffee.

MADELEINE: We're not going to have another scene, are we?

DAVID: We? Have another scene?

MADELEINE: Because I know full well that whenever a person offers another person a cup of coffee, a scene is sure to follow.

DAVID: That's only in soap operas.

MADELEINE: You mean daytime serials?

DAVID: A rose by any other name . . . That's Shakespeare.

MADELEINE: What a good idea for a soap! We have these families, see, from different sides of the tracks, and the girl from one family falls in love with the boy from the other. I envision this terribly romantic scene with her in her nightgown out on a balcony, and he comes into the garden and sees her in the moonlight—

DAVID: It's been done.

MADELEINE: Spoilsport. That needn't stop us. Every plot idea in the world has been used at least once in every soap.

DAVID: Now *you're* calling them soaps.

MADELEINE: Well, I've been thinking, David. A person can be too sensitive. I've come to terms with the term. It's time we stopped feeling guilty about soaps. They are what they are, poor successful, attractive, underrated dears.

DAVID: Oh, Mad. I can tell from that sparkle in your eyes, you're in love. Would you like to tell me about it?

MADELEINE: Oh, yes, yes, David . . . You're always near when I need you, old friend.

DAVID: Sit down and have a cup of coffee.

So there it is, the world of soap, its lives and its loves, its manners, morals, and makers. But we cannot tune out Pepper Young and Helen Trent, Mrs. Carrington and the Hummerts, Phil Holden, Joanne Tate, and Bernice Robinson just yet. They have been with us too long, taken too much of our time, played too much on our emotions, to be dismissed without An Appreciation.

Yet what, after all, can be said? As soaps approach the half-century mark their identity is clear. They have evolved into a very definite, instantly recognizable form with conventions of its own and an audience apparently satisfied with exactly what soap opera has come to be. Yet respectability seems forever beyond the grasp of soaps. Their very name is derisive. Nobody calls a daytime serial a daytime serial. Soaps they are, and soaps they will remain.

In all history, there has never been an art form, popular or pure, that has been subjected to such censorious scrutiny. Others have been more passionately denounced and dramatically vilified—modern music, for instance, or nonobjective art—but none so unremittingly and witheringly scorned.

Soaps have been scolded, and still are, for being too glossy and unreal. In the eyes of sophisticates, they have replaced religion as the opiate of the masses. They are poorly written, simple-minded, sentimental. They are scored for not instructing their audiences about the issues of the day and the problems of the real world.

Almost the only people who have anything good to say about soaps are those who make money from them—writers, actors and producers, advertisers and broadcasting companies. And even they are frequently apologetic or defensive about their association.

Then, of course, there is the audience, which keeps tuning in tomorrow and tomorrow and tomorrow. Certainly here one might expect the loud vote of affirmation. Yet even here there is a curious reluctance to stand foursquare for soaps. It is almost as though the critics—numerous, assertive and self-confident—have convinced the audience that nice people don't tune in to soaps or, if you can imagine such a thing, that soaps are un-American.

For that last bit of criticism, we must turn back to the beginning, to Dr. Louis Berg, the first to make his name by hating soaps. Dr. Berg had always maintained that soap opera helped women immerse themselves in unwholesome fantasy, sealing themselves away from reality in a morbid dreamworld built around their own frustrations. But from there he went on to warn of darker things. Those pernicious serials, he averred, were exactly what the Axis Powers wanted the American housewife to listen to. The "state of anxiety" soaps create, he said, is the "very same overanxiety which is the end of all enemy propaganda, for it lays the groundwork for civilian panic in emergencies and saps the productive energies of the afflicted individuals in all their essential efforts." Strong words, these, to pile atop all his other accusations—that soap opera caused such alarming symptoms as arrhythmia, tachycardia, vertigo, and high blood pressure.

But something as profitable as soap opera is not spiritlessly abandoned in the face of criticism, from Dr. Berg or anyone else. So the networks were soon at work mobilizing a counterattack. They began to subsidize—though, of course, as they were careful to point out, in no way to influence—social scientists, anthropologists, physicians, and psychiatrists of their own to study soap opera, its listeners, and the effects of the former upon the latter, in the hope that somehow the reputations of such ladies as Helen Trent, Big Sister, and Our Gal Sunday might be salvaged.

They could. The reports that began to flow from the presses differed only in their diagnosis of what particular benefits serials were bringing into the life of the American housewife and how they achieved their beneficial effects.

One group demonstrated that the devotees of *Big Sister*, a very popular serial with a heroine most of its listeners strongly identified with, were ordinarily bothered by depression and the feeling that they had little control over their own lives. This sinking feeling was brought on not by serial addiction, as Dr. Berg might have suggested, but by the fact that middle-class stay-at-home wives and mothers felt themselves powerless and at the mercy of their husbands' every change of mood and fortune. They suffered particularly from the fear that, as dependent wives, they might have a very hard time indeed if their husbands were to abandon them, as sometimes seemed likely. But since they identified with Ruth Wayne, the strong heroine who so effectively managed to cope with problems far greater than theirs, these women felt an increased sense of personal adequacy and control—as measured by psychological tests.

Another study group announced, in suitably academic prose, that any shortcomings the serials might have were heavily outweighed by their virtues. "Since the tendency of all the dramas studied is toward the solutions that are generally accepted as ethical in our social existence," the researchers proclaimed, "the effects of the dramas tend toward helpfulness rather than harm." They warned, however, that "the creators of the daytime serial must always keep in mind the great psychological power of suggestions, particularly to avoid all abnormal behaviorism. Good taste would indicate the common sense of this approach if there were no psychiatric hazards. Our preliminary investigations show little cause for alarm on this score, but we feel it wise to indicate the positive role in inspiration and encouragement that the radio drama can play. Obviously the negative elements of life have little value." Dr. Berg's reaction to this description of the soaps' inspirational role is not recorded.

Another survey tried to find out who was actually listening to the serials. Had Dr. Berg been correct in suggesting that it was a legion of neurotics and hypochondriacal sadists? The researchers studies 5030 housewives in 125 communities, from city to farm. Fifty-four per cent turned out to be serial fans. The average listener tuned in for one hour and twenty-seven minutes a day; she followed 5.8 different programs, tuning in each one 2.5 times a week. Forty per cent of college women were fans, as were 35 per cent of all those in the highest economic level.

Not only were they fans, but many were true believers too. "Do you believe the serial is true to life?" the survey asked, and it included two very favorable responses among the answers to be checked off: "I recognize myself in this serial, either as I am or as I would like to be," and "This really could happen. It seems to be believable." Seventy-five per cent of the whole group and 59 per cent of those with high school or college education said yes to one of these.

Nobody seemed able to discover anything that set the serial listeners apart from the ladies who did not listen. They all went to church and movies, read magazines, and engaged in social activities at about the same rate. Dr. Berg to the contrary notwithstanding, there was no recognizable type of serial listener.

When the results of this study were released—especially the startling finding that 40 per cent of college-educated women were listening to soap opera—all heck broke loose. A survey was promptly taken at Wells College in California, and it concluded that "Wells girls have a healthy contempt for the sugar-coated unrealities of daytime serials and cannot understand why any college woman in her right mind should bother listening to them." The English department at Mount Holyoke in Massachusetts, queried on the network-sponsored survey, found comfort in the fact that 60 per cent of college-educated women were *not* listening to serials. As for their personal view, the teachers sniffed that the soaps were "characteristic of the prevailing vulgarity of our time."

Here and there special groups were organizing and working themselves into a lather over soaps. Such groups suggested not only that the shows were unwholesome—since they dealt with such themes as murder, insanity, medical operations, jealousy, broken hearts, indifferent husbands, and mother-in-law trouble—but that they were not even what listeners really wanted. One group collected statistics to show that most daytime programing consisted of serials, but that only 7 per cent of the listening audience wanted them.

In 1946 the FCC joined the critics, suggesting that broadcasting companies correct their deplorable practice of "piling up" soap operas during the morning. Retreating immediately to the favorite refuge of a frightened broadcaster, the National Association of Broadcasters accused the FCC of launching an attack on freedom of speech, "a reversion to that type of government control and regulation which our forefathers struggled to escape." The FCC suggestion, NAB claimed, "reveals a desire to impose artificial and arbitrary controls over what the people of this country shall hear." It piously proclaimed the broadcasters "the champions of the people in resisting both direct and indirect encroachment of government upon the freedom of speech."

Undeterred, the FCC continued to nag the soaps. In March 1948 the agency was pleased to announce that three fourths of the available radio audience were keeping their sets off during soap hours. The most popular soap had only 12.5 per cent of the available audience.

While this conflict continued at the highest levels, most people considered soaps too far down on the scale of human culture even to merit discussion. Their contempt colored the attitude of soap writers and actors, who were often embarrassed by their own profession. Mary Jane Higby, star of *When a Girl Marries,* says she "felt reluctant to say what it was I did for a living" because "the serials were in such bad repute." Anne Hummert herself, aware of the disdain in which the daytime serial was held, admitted to an interviewer that her young son, John Ashenhurst, also disapproved of her specialty. "As a matter of fact," she told the reporter, "I sit behind my desk with two black eyes."

A few radio soaps that were felt to be somehow of a finer nature than the rest were excepted from the general scorn and condescension. Sandra Michael's *Lone Journey* and *Against the Storm* were the most acclaimed. Only fragments of the scripts are available, so no one can presume to assess their merits fairly. But one may perhaps be excused for doubting that they regularly scaled the literary heights claimed for them by nostalgic admirers. An example of the way *Lone Journey* "rounded off the day's drama in exquisite manner" suggests that it has been oversold:

"Henry's voice echoed happily in the still, cold air. Sydney left her baking and came hurrying out of the house, and together they stood listening for the faraway sound of Mel's car. Soon from the direction of the Double Spear T came the signal of several short, cheerful blasts of the car horn.

"Sydney and her Uncle Henry smiled and nodded quickly. Wolfe had come home. In a bare tree just beyond the porch, Mr. Olsen, the magpie, scolded in jealous annoyance at not being noticed. Sydney ran into the house and came back to give him an outrageously big helping of his favorite feed. Holiday warmth and excitement spread in great waves, from the oven within doors, to include the yard, the ranch, and the whole valley under the peaceful sky of a November afternoon."

And what comment is possible on this scrap of its sister program, *Against the Storm*? Kathy, a refugee, has a dream in which soldiers killed in World War II live again and recognize that, despite past enmity, all men are brothers. A friend, Phil, appears in her dream.

PHIL: This is a dream, Kathy. You are dreaming.

KATHY: Yes, I know . . . but will they be welcome? Those soldiers are muddy and covered with blood . . . American . . . Russian . . . German . . .

PHIL: Look. You see, Kathy?

KATHY: They have come to the houses!

PHIL: You see? The first one knocked . . .

KATHY: And the door was opened! They are welcome!

PHIL: And don't think they're somber guests on Christmas morning, Kathy. No one should be afraid to think of them today . . . not because we can forget that they died for us, but we can also remember that they lived, and even those who were brutalized and poisoned by Nazism once could have had it in them, like the others, like our own beloved dead, to love life and their fellow men . . . They could have laughed and sung with the others . . . and as the others want all the world to sing and laugh in the future.

KATHY: Listen, Philip . . . is it the soldiers laughing?

PHIL: I think it is. Let's remember them that way—the soldiers, the men and women and children who with their own lives have brought song and laughter for us and for the new world to come. Remember, and welcome them to our hearts today and forever!

This program became so intellectually respectable that it was able to present Edgar Lee Masters reading from *The Spoon River Anthology*. John Masefield was shortwaved in from England for one episode, in which he was supposed to be lecturing and reading from his own work to the class of Professor Allen, a leading character. Such a high tone prevailed during this episode that no commercials were used that day. Even President Roosevelt accepted an invitation to appear on the show, although his appearance was canceled when World War II supervened.

The other soap that was truly respectable as well as widely respected was *One Man's Family,* written by Carleton E. Morse. It never introduced any of the violence and crime so common in other soaps, possibly because Morse, who also chronicled the adventures of Jack, Doc, and Reggie on *I Love a Mystery,* was using his aggressive invention elsewhere.

One Man's Family told the story of the Barbours, who lived in the Seacliff section of San Francisco. It was "dedicated to the younger generation and their bewildering offspring." Its respectability was heavily underlined by its organization into chapters and books, rather than mere nameless episodes, as well as by its time slot, a half hour on Sundays. For most of its life it was a weekly show, though in 1950 it was demoted to fifteen-minute daily life. The last broadcast, in 1959, was chapter 30 of book 134, and there had been, in all, 3256 episodes. This means that *One Man's Family* spanned more years than any other soap, and the audience to whom it had seemed an unalterable fact of life mourned it sincerely.

So did its author. Morse wrote the show's obituary in the Los Angeles *Times*. "My own sorrow," he said, "is not so much in the cessation of the show as such as in the thought that one more happy, sober beacon to light the way has been put out . . . The signposts for sound family life are now few, and I feel the loss of *One Man's Family* is just another abandoned lighthouse."

Morse's views on the importance of family life had frequently been made clear on the program itself. In 1938 Father Barbour put it this way: "It's my opinion that the family is the source from whence comes the moral strength of a nation. And disintegration of any nation begins with the disintegration of the family. The family is the smallest unit in society. Millions and millions of these little units make a nation. And the standards of living set up by these family units indicate the high or low standards of a nation . . . A well-disciplined, morally upright family is bound to turn out good citizens! Good citizens make a good nation."

To this, one of his grown sons replied, "No doubt about that! There's a rising tide of sentiment growing throughout the world, fostered by people who are sick over the way things are going . . . Perhaps it's the answer we've all been looking for . . . an answer in the hearts of men."

Such sentiments would not, perhaps, thrill the listener, but they might produce a warm and satisfying moral glow. Even Dr. Berg could find nothing to complain of.

It is difficult to rank soaps on literary excellence, since they are not often reviewed and most scripts have not been preserved. But it is certain that some of the soaps, varying from year to year as writers changed, have been as well written as any serious drama on television. As an example of writing quite different from what most people would associate with soap opera, consider this ending from a program never cited as an example of literary distinction, *Ma Perkins.*

MA: Shuffle, if we'll only look around us, we'll see so much to—to take the sting out of our sorrows! That's what I meant when I waved my hand at Rushville Center. At Mr. Johnson raking his leaves. And the smell of the October leaves being burned on twenty lawns and the yellow house lights blinking on as folks like us walk home after a day's work. Living . . . I guess what I'm talking about is living. Taking the days as they come . . . the seasons . . . living for each day itself . . . just living! Putting up the screens in May and taking 'em down in September . . . doing your work, listening on an October night to the wild geese, as a mile over our heads they go on their wonderful and mysterious journey!

SHUFFLE: Yep . . . that sure is a wonderful sound.

MA: You know, Shuffle, when I was a little girl, my father used to stand with me outside our house, of an October afternoon, and show me the wild birds going south. Looked sort of like a smoky smudge. And one year—I must have been six or so—a gray goose feather fell right at my feet. And my father laughed, and he said, "Hold on to that, young lady, the bird'll be back in the spring to get it, or maybe to drop you another feather!" And I asked my father—somehow it impressed me—"Year after year, will that same goose be flying over our house?" He smiled sadly, and said, "If you'll be here to find the feather, the goose will drop it for you." [*A tiny pause.*] I'm a woman grown, but I've never forgotten that little incident. And ever since I've *liked* the idea of year after year . . . the regularity of the seasons . . . the mysterious way of God, moving those birds across a thousand miles of day and night and empty air, and me standing there, a part of it, because I . . . well, because I'm a part of it. And that's what I'd like my children to know . . . especially Fay . . . I'd like *her* to see that if we'll only be there to find it, the gray goose feather will always come. Telling us that the world goes on . . .

SHUFFLE [*quietly; he's deeply moved*]: I guess that's the story of our lives, Ma . . . the lives of you and me and the rest of us who stay in all the forgotten little villages, and let the rest of the world go by. Except . . . *we* don't let the world go by . . . it's the folks in a hurry who let it by. Us, we got time to take it in.

MA [*not much volume but very earnest*]: Yes, Shuffle . . . that's it exactly! And that's the secret of peace. Let each day come . . . take it as it comes . . . take it for everything it has . . . and when it goes you've lived that day!

Soaps are sometimes damned with faint praise by critics who are quite ready to concede that the production, acting, and casting can be excellent—but go on to deplore the waste of all that talent on such unpromising material. Most of the really trenchant criticism, however, is aimed not at soap opera the literary form but at soap opera the social influence. What soaps teach, or fail to teach, is the issue. This kind of criticism often comes from people who have spent one day assessing the genre and indignantly report their findings, like tourists repudiating Manhattan after a visit to Times Square.

One literary lady who devoted a New Year's Day in the mid-forties to her analysis of radio soaps reported that "they would have women believe that falling in and out of love, solving personal problems, is the end-all and be-all of a woman's life." What she would have liked them to do instead becomes clear as she continues. "I would never have known there are such things as labor-management strife, reconversion problems, returned veterans at loose ends, a critical housing shortage, discrimination against minorities, the atom bomb, and an uneasy unity among the great nations. I would not even have known there had been a war going on, except for a few casual references to men characters just out of uniform."

Worst of all, apparently, was the fact that soap opera had no expert guidance to offer its listeners on international relations. When they extended their New Year's greeting, the critical lady complained, "All of the heroines exhorted the radio audience 'to make true peace a reality.'" But—and now comes the indictment—"I gathered no hint, through a long day of listening, how the miracle of peace might specifically be achieved."

This insistence that soaps rush in, first to solve and then to explain the larger social problems for their audience, has persisted. Some critics condemn soap opera because it "teaches a kind of pernicious individualism." Soap problems, they complain, are brought about by human duplicity and weakness —and, although they fail to note it, solved by human strength and understanding—rather than by impersonal stresses in society. Soaps, by their insistence on a personal explanation of events, fail to add to audience understanding of the economic and social forces that govern so large a part of real life. World population vis-à-vis food supply, the causes of war, monetary systems, the possibility of world government, all go unrecorded and unexplained by the soaps.

For all this criticism, no one has ever explained just why soap opera is obligated to become the vehicle of instruction about great social and economic forces, or why this educational responsibility should not be taken on by movies, plays, or novels. The popular song and the comic book come close to soap opera in drawing critical fire. For example, objections are often raised to the use of terms from the drug culture in various song lyrics; the lower nature of adolescents has, it is said, been musically encouraged by jazz or rock; and comic books have been blamed for nightmares both real and figurative, including crimes of violence. But neither popular music nor the comics have been seriously informed that it is their responsibility to bring enlightenment about the great social forces to the darkened minds of the masses.

Some comics have risen unbidden to the challenge, managing to snip *Hamlet* and *Moby Dick* to their measure; and the form has been adopted by would-be preachers of the Good, the True, and the Beautiful who, knowing that any cartoon is likely to be at least cursorily read, have used them to get across the message about causes ranging from birth control to voting registration. The popular song found a vocation of a different kind: it was taken up and brilliantly adapted to the purposes of commercialism. Some of the most memorable songs on radio and television are sung not about love or drugs or death, but about a soft drink, a dog food, or an airline.

But the real comic books, the real comic strips, the real popular songs, continue on their way unchanged. They have not accepted the idea that it is up to them to bring the message of truth. They are what they are.

The soaps, on the other hand, have meekly listened to the complaint that they fail to accept their responsibility as educators, and they have tried to mend their ways. True, they have not undertaken an extended analysis of the complex social forces underlying the American way of life and world affairs, but there is certainly a large area of social service—usually involving personal behavior—within which the soaps feel a very definite sense of mission.

It was during World War II that the soap opera accepted its role as advertiser of unimpeachably worthy causes. By that time it had become evident that soaps wielded enormous power. A program that could draw truckloads of presents for a leading character's wedding, or induce four hundred thousand listeners to enter a contest to rename an imaginary horse, was obviously one that carried weight with its listeners.

Thus wartime government enlisted soaps as allies on the home front. Soon characters on almost every program were deep in war work, if not battle itself. Male characters were wounded, sometimes killed, in action. Patriotism was a major topic of conversation, as were the saving of fat and tinfoil, and the purchase of war bonds. *Bachelor's Children* was broadcast in Spanish to Latin America to increase hemispheric solidarity. Sometimes real war heroes or high Army officers were introduced into soap episodes, to spur patriotic feeling or to sell bonds. Eleanor Roosevelt herself suggested a bond purchase during an episode of *The Story of Bess Johnson,* and soap opera heroines used the rapport they had established with their audiences to help the cause.

In one typical appeal, the announcer has just wound up the commercial. "And now," he says, "back to Procter & Gamble's story of *Rosemary.*" We hear ten seconds of theme music, which is interrupted by the voice of Rosemary Dawson, the show's leading character.

ROSEMARY: Oh, Ed—just a minute—just a minute—

DARLINGTON: What is it, Rosemary?

ROSEMARY: I want to say something before the show starts—

DARLINGTON: Well, this is most unusual—

ROSEMARY: I know it is, but I have an unusual request to make—

DARLINGTON: All right, go ahead, but don't take too long.

ROSEMARY: I won't. I am speaking to you—all of you—my friends out there, listening to *Rosemary*—I am speaking to the mothers and wives and sweethearts of our men who are fighting to bring this war to a close—to make this a free world—the kind of world you want to live in—the kind of a world we Dawsons want to live in . . . If you will do something for me, I'll do something for you. If you'll buy a war bond—because I, Rosemary Dawson, ask you to—and send me the receipt showing me you have purchased it—I shall return that receipt with a personal letter from me. I am doing this because I want so much to make the Seventh War Loan Drive the biggest drive we have ever had. And so will you, my dear friends, who have listened to and enjoyed this program—who have laughed with us and cried with us—buy a war bond—or as many bonds as you can—and send your receipt to Rosemary Dawson, care of *Rosemary*, to this station, and you will receive a letter from me and my thanks. Now, Ed, you can take over.

Welfare groups and government agencies were eager to cooperate with soap opera writers in return for their participation in the war effort. They offered instruction and advice, suggesting such themes as the betterment of race relations (to ease tensions in the Army) and the importance of learning what to do in a medical emergency (in case the war reached American soil). One prominent soap writer was proud to let it be known that before plotting a show she consulted with the American Legion, the American Medical Association, the Association for Family Living, the Federal Council of Churches of Christ in America, the National Education Association, the Navy Department, the Office of War Information, the Red Cross, the Veterans Administration, and the War Department.

After the war, government pressure relaxed and race relations were discarded as a soap theme, not to be revived for many years, but soap opera writers continued to concern themselves with good works, albeit those of a less controversial nature. They presented the problems of returning veterans and POWs, and appealed for money to help worthy causes. Sometimes they worked their charities into the story. A visit by Rosemary and her mother to a young couple who have just had their first child provided a good opportunity for one such effort.

LARRY: I don't remember ever being so happy.

ANNA: Nor I—and grateful, too—grateful that we have a son—a healthy, wonderful little boy.

MOTHER: Yes, dear, you should be grateful for that.

LARRY: I—I've been thinking about that—about how lucky we are—and I'd like to be able to do something to show our gratitude. I'd like to contribute to some—some good cause in the baby's name.

ANNA: Oh, I'd like that, too, Larry. Please—let's do it.

ROSEMARY: Well, I'll tell you of a good cause if you're looking for one.

LARRY: What do you suggest?

ROSEMARY: It seems to me that a contribution to the Easter Seal Campaign for the care and treatment of crippled children would be appropriate at this time.

ANNA: I—I—hate to think of them, Rosemary, when my baby, thank God, is healthy and strong.

ROSEMARY: Which is exactly why you should think of those poor unfortunate others. That's one of the reasons you should want to help them. And you can, by buying Easter Seals—to help expand treatment and training of these children.

LARRY: Thanks, Rosemary, I'm going to make out a check right now—right this minute.

ROSEMARY: Good for you.

ANNA: And make it a generous check, Larry, as generous as possible for us.

LARRY: I will, honey. It's one way we can show how thankful we are that our baby's healthy. Maybe in this way we can help somebody else's child to run and to play in the good free air of this country!

This feeling of responsibility to preach the unexceptionable persists in today's soaps, and writers are prompt to adduce examples of meritorious social service at the first breath of criticism or disapproval from outside the soap world.

One program undertook a five-month campaign to educate its viewers about the Pap test. The heroine of the show was afflicted with uterine cancer, which, detected at an early stage, proved curable. The audience took the lesson to heart and went for a Pap test; the mail the program reaped from this demonstrated, to the writer's satisfaction, at least, that it had been instrumental in saving thousands of lives.

The soaps have crusaded busily against drug abuse and venereal disease. Genuine young addicts have been shown in the course of their treatment. A character on one show was integrated into a group therapy session at a rehabilitation center, and the viewing youth of America were presumably sobered and chastened while their parents were alerted to the dangers that might lie ahead.

The venereal disease campaigners did not leave audience response to conjecture. They tested the reaction to their work by having a young reporter character on the show write an article on VD. This article, "Venereal Disease: A Fact We Must Face and Fight," was offered to anyone who wanted to write in for it. Over ten thousand people did.

Other programs have dealt at length with the readjustment problems of people released from mental institutions, thereby encouraging tolerance and understanding and preaching the efficacy of psychiatry. The danger of carbon monoxide poisoning in the home was emphasized for the audience of another show. Even race relations have been brought to the fore again, notably by one program that tried to explain to the audience why a young, beautiful (and very light) Negro woman might choose to pass as white: she had been rejected in youth, it seems, by both black and white communities. Black characters are being conscientiously introduced on several shows, though it has been snidely whispered that all of them are paragons of middle-class virtue and not in the least interested in inter-racial marriages.

Soaps, then, have taken the highest available moral ground, but their critics continue nonetheless to carp. Soaps, they say, are not dealing with real life. The problems the characters face are too highly colored, too dramatic, too unlikely. Why, they ask, do the soaps avoid real problems of the sort the audience themselves presumably confront in their own daily lives—say, a dispute between husband and wife about whether the family should vacation in the mountains or at the seashore, or whether the wife should take a part-time job?

One sharp-eyed critic has figured out the answer: the advertisers are behind it all. Unscrupulous sponsors, she avers, insist that soap opera continue to foster the daydreaming state of mind that allows their commercial messages to make a deeper impression. These sponsors, the argument runs, will never permit soap opera to deal with real-life problems, since the critical faculties must be lulled to sleep by the housewife's continuing participation in a never-never land of sudsy fantasy. If soap opera dealt with real problems (the part-time job controversy, say) it would put the housewife into quite a different state of receptivity. Unlulled by fantasy, she would bring her critical thought and judgment to bear on the commercial message and reject it. Thus advertisers must dedicate themselves to the struggle to keep the curtains drawn, shutting out the cold light of the real world, lest the necessary fantasy foam be dissipated.

This analysis, with a mistrust of the audience worthy of Dr. Berg himself, is tinctured with mild paranoia, depending on the concept of an omniscient and Svengalian sponsor who can manipulate the audience mind to suit his every whim. It also seems to depend on a misconception of why the house-wife watches one show rather than another. Surely it is not because she yearns to be softened up for a commercial message, but because she likes what she is getting. The sponsor, in turn, buys the opportunity to speak to her between the acts. The sponsor's interest, then, lies in holding an audience by offering what it wants.

It doesn't seem likely that sponsors fear the serialization of real-life problems because it might hone the intelligence to so fine a critical edge that the audience would instantaneously reject the commercial. Rather, and legitimately, sponsors fear that their audiences might simply disappear. The continued depiction of realistic trivia and practical problems might well induce the audience to turn the dial to other channels in search of more gripping fare.

The subject matter suggested as appropriate for the new, better, truly realistic soap opera would be numbingly dull even if the protagonists were one's own friends, neighbors, or family. Who cares if Mrs. Simmons down the block takes that part-time job? It might engage our interest more fully if we knew that the fate of the Simmons marriage hung precariously in the balance. And the part-time job would probably excite us thoroughly if we thought that by accepting it Mrs. Simmons would be thrown into daily proximity with her former lover, Dr. Joe Smith, who is actually the father of the Simmonses' little Danny.

Nor is this mere hypothesis. In 1943 a radio show called *Brave Tomorrow* actually tried the experiment of dealing realistically with less than cataclysmic conflicts. It told the story of a young wife following her husband from Army base to Army base while he waited to be sent overseas, facing problems of such unassailable realism that the major one was her inability to obtain the set of dishes her heart was set on. Before the show was taken off the air, it had reduced the sponsor's representative to such a state of frustration that he wired the producer: FOR GOD'S SAKE, TELL HER THERE IS STILL SEARS, ROEBUCK!

Everyone who writes about soap opera offers advice about how it could be improved, and manages to list a number of defects that should prevent anyone (except perhaps the bedridden deaf) from watching it. It is interesting, then, to wonder why the people who write so critically about soaps continue to watch them. Of course, for some the reason is simple: they watch as a scientist might observe the growth of a new bacillus, and their descriptions of what they see are intended to cure the rest of us. But some of the critics most eloquent in condemnation have clearly been watching (or listening to) soaps for years, on their own time, unassigned to such duty, and unpaid. Why?

One explains that she started because she thought that something watched by so many people must have social significance, and she wanted to understand it. After a while, however, she decided that her reason for watching was that soaps rest the tired brain. After a hard morning of creativity, a gentle brainwashing is in order. She paradoxically claims that she values the soaps not despite but because of their pervasive unreality. If one listens to music, she says, one must think; everything in life exacts some reaction—except soap opera, which floats one gently into a mindless realm where everything is unreal, unending, meaningless.

Another intellectual lady who sometimes sharpens her pen on soaps does not attempt to explain her own obviously long viewing history, but she does at some length consider the motivation of others. The real audience, she concludes, is watching because soaps present a view of life with which they thoroughly agree. This shared view of life is one of "a bitter, sad, dangerous ordeal," and the audience recognizes that the stories are truthfully describing the misery, isolation, hatred, desperation, and despair that make up the inner reality of their own existence. To this critic, sustained morbidity and dread, daily, inexorable, and almost unrelieved depression are the message and appeal of soaps.

In passing, she wonders why it is that everyone's memories of such old-time radio soap characters as Helen Trent should be so strong and vivid to this day. "Surely," she admits, "we could not have been sick, or otherwise home from school, on so very many mornings, and 'amnesia' need not have been our first word of adult pathology." But she never attempts to deal with the question. Why indeed, if soaps purvey nothing but unrelieved depression, morbidity, etc., would so many people, including our critic, follow them with interest? Can there be such a constant streak of masochism in their psyches that they must pursue it wherever it leads in an eager quest for new and varied miseries? And do pain and agony really form the bond between the soaps and their audience?

Surely something is being offered by soaps to their audience that goes far beyond a desire for psychic discomfort, or even gentle brainwashing. Traditionally there are two main reasons why people follow soaps. One is to escape from everyday life; the other is to learn to cope with it more effectively. These two motives are not so different as they may sound. Some of the lessons of soap are learned consciously; some, perhaps the larger ones, are offered through fantasy and absorbed on an unconscious level.

Soaps, of course, have always made an effort to offer their audiences valuable moral content in addition to pure entertainment. This applies not only to their advocacy of such causes as Easter Seals and driving safety; it applies, more importantly, to the moral truths, both great and small, that are taught by the heroes and heroines of soap, by example and by advice that can be taken to heart and later brought to bear on the problems of the real world.

There is a great deal to be learned from soaps about how

to handle one's life and one's close relationships. Everyone in the audience is necessarily limited in his knowledge of how other people really live. Only soap opera purports to offer a detailed day-by-day demonstration of the way others behave in intimate situations.

Soaps show their audiences how young lovers talk to each other after a long separation, how a wife reacts to the discovery of her husband's infidelity, how a couple quarrel and then forgive. Where else can the audience learn how other parents advise their children about marriage, how deeply one friend questions another about his wife's alcoholism, how much a father tells his daughter about his divorce?

But beyond this education in intimacy, soaps exert a far more profound influence on their audiences. Most forms of entertainment—bowling, quiz shows, bridge—are morally neutral. They make no attempt to raise questions of meaning and value. Soaps, on the other hand, have always addressed themselves primarily to exactly these questions. The situations and events dealt with by the soaps force the viewer to consider and answer some of the time-honored philosophical questions: What is happiness? What is love? How can we reconcile ourselves to misfortune, accept death, justify what seems like a crushing and incomprehensible fate? What do we live for anyway? And is it all worthwhile?

If the unexamined life is not worth living, these are important questions. We may disapprove the manner of their asking, find the stories that embody them simplistic and even vulgar. When the answers come, we may not like them, either. But the soaps are providing at least an attempt to find meaning in individual life, and it is from this attempt that they gain their energy and magnetism.

The unhappiness many people see as central to soap opera is the key to this basic appeal. Though sustained misery is not really characteristic of the form, sustained anxiety is. Soap opera people agonize over decisions, and worry about what the results of their actions will be. Should Barbara marry Tony when she is not sure she loves him? Should Tara tell Chuck who is the father of her unborn child? Should Rosemary risk marrying a man who has lost his memory and may be already married? The intense emotional energy expended on these decisions reflects not a morbid commitment to depression but the depth of the characters' belief in the importance of the individual life.

Women's liberationists protest the soaps' view of women as eternally preoccupied with personal emotional problems. These are the traditionally feminine concerns of the old-fashioned, unliberated woman. Today's women, they claim, should not seek satisfaction in domestic and subservient wife and mother roles; in order to reflect the true values of today's liberated society, Soapland's women should be shown forging careers, budgeting their money, and otherwise meeting the challenges of equality.

But the central message of soaps should not offend the feminists, whether they agree with it or not. It never suggests that men find their most lasting satisfactions in career and conflict, while women must be content to seek theirs at sink, ironing board, and bassinet. Rather, it powerfully demonstrates that the individual life—which is to say the small, restricted, essentially domestic life—is the field on which everything that really matters, for man or woman, comes to focus and is won or lost. The only life that can bring happiness is the life of the heart—of emotional commitment to other people. Soaps tell us that the problems men have traditionally confronted, to succeed or fail, are unimportant, superficial, irrelevant to the central concerns of life. Satisfaction is simply not to be found by anyone in the traditionally masculine pursuits. Far from suggesting a double standard, or a division of life into male and female specialties, soaps utterly reject conventional masculine values, holding up conventional feminine values in their place as the only desirable standard.

And who is to say that this message should not be listened to? In an increasingly impersonal, computerized, and mobile society, much of what people do is dictated by the circumstances of their jobs, their life-styles, and their obligations. Perhaps the soaps, a sustained cry for the primacy of feeling in life, provide an invaluable reminder to their audience.

There will continue to be critics, numerous and vehement, who disagree, but there must be something in a form, art or not, that lasts so long and attracts so many. It is as much an expression of American culture as skyscrapers and superhighways and hot-dog stands. To be sure, there are many who do not like skyscrapers and superhighways or even hot dogs. But they will not disappear simply because someone finds them distasteful. One may ignore soaps, but to do so is to pass up a chance to glimpse the mind and mood of a large segment of America. Middle America, perhaps, and perhaps not worthy of serious consideration when Art is up for discussion. But it is well to remember that every culture has its mythology, created by nameless men and women, many of them illiterate, passed down and altered from one generation to another, used to create imperishable masterpieces, whip up patriotic enthusiasm for dubious enterprises, or frighten children into good behavior. Disavow them as we will, the soaps are our own American mythology.

DAVID: Well, that's the last of the coffee.

MADELEINE: We'll just have to stop, then. The party's over. I see the sun is just rising over the RCA Building. Let's pack up.

DAVID: Who gets to keep the coffee urn?

MADELEINE: Ssh! Not in front of the a-u-d-i-e-n-c-e. We'll talk about it in the elevator. Come along. Don't forget the manuscript for the book.

DAVID: What book?

MADELEINE: *The* book. *Our* book. *The Soaps.*

DAVID: Oh, yeah. What would I ever do without you, Mad?

MADELEINE: We'll discuss that in the elevator too.

[MADELEINE *and* DAVID *are at the door now. They turn for one last, lingering, affectionate look at the deserted office where so many hours of their young lives have so recently been spent. Hours of joy and sorrow, laughter and tears, problems and peace.*]

DAVID: It's been fun, hasn't it?

MADELEINE: You're really somethin', David. Did you know that?

DAVID: And you, Mad, are somethin' else.

[*She turns off the lights. They are now lit only by the faint, warm glow of the rising sun, silhouetted in the doorway. She smiles, then speaks.*]

MADELEINE: David-pal, did you ever think of becoming a writer in real life?

[DAVID *looks as if he is about to speak but the door closes and* MADELEINE, *as usual, has had the last word as we go to black.*]

INDEX

§